EUROPEAN COMMISSION

CARING FOR OUR FUTURE

2nd edition

ACTION FOR EUROPE'S ENVIRONMENT

25 ISSUES AT A GLANCE

Brussels - Luxembourg - 1998

CARING FOR OUR FUTURE

ACTION FOR EUROPE'S ENVIRONMENT

Published by

Office for Official Publications
of the European Communities
Luxembourg, 1998

Editor

European Commission
Directorate-General XI
Environment, Nuclear Safety
and Civil Protection

With the support of
European Environment Agency, Copenhagen

Layout

Paquet & Cléda

Translation

CT Belgium s.a.

Editorial work

Newcom s.a.

Additional information
on the environment is available
on the Internet.
It can be accessed through
the Europa server :
http://europa.eu.int/en/comm/
dg11/dg11home.html.
and
http://www.eea.eu.int/

Office for Official Publications
of the European Communities,
Luxembourg, 1998
ISBN 92-828-2889-1
©European Communities, 1998
Cat. n° CR-11-98-851-EN-C

Clearer understanding
means more effective action!

I t's now more than 25 years since Europe began to concern itself with the environment. A long time in some respects, but a short one when it comes to developing a policy capable of tackling the huge challenges on which our future and that of our children depends.

We don't always appreciate precisely what is at stake. There are many different parties involved in preparing and implementing this policy. Technically, the issues are complex and the tools we have at our disposal, are continually being improved and updated. Keeping citizens fully informed is a vital element of European environmental policy. Public awareness has to be raised if we are to persuade citizens to help protect and manage our environment.

The present publication is designed to meet precisely these needs. Countless technical studies and reports already exist, not to mention collections of laws and other specialist publications. We believe, however, that there is a clear need for a book that brings the issues together in a way that is accessible to all. The aim of this publication is to provide the general reader with a review of the current state of our environment and the measures taken in this field at European level. We hope it will enable citizens to form a critical view of their own actions, the issues at stake and the precise responsibility of each player.

The book has been produced with the invaluable support of the European Environment Agency. For each theme, the reader is first presented with the principal facts and trends, based on our current knowledge. These are followed by a brief discussion of the actions taken by European institutions and by a review of proposals currently under discussion. The final part of each section examines individual players and their responsibility in the relevant field. The way the book is structured also highlights the links that exist between the different themes.

I hope that this book will show how far we have come over the past quarter of a century and that it will encourage people to take an active part on the road yet to be travelled. A clearer understanding can help us all act more responsibly.

Ritt BJERREGAARD
European Commissioner for the Environment, Civil Protection and Nuclear Safety

TABLE OF CONTENTS

TABLE OF CONTENTS

his work provides information on a central document comprising 25 factsheets relating to different environmental issues.

This work can therefore be consulted according to your information needs. The division between one type of information and another is marked using a system of icons (logos).

STRUCTURE

The work comprises four sections:

1. The central document
2. Glossary
3. Bibliography
4. Timeline

1. The central document

Comprises 25 factsheets, each dealing with a particular environmental topic.

Each issue is depicted in an icon. The list of environmental issues and their corresponding icons is repeated in the index and in the table of contents. They are also listed on the bookmark attached to this work.

For each issue tackled, this central document provides information on:

- facts and trends;
- European Union actions; and
- the responsibilities of the various players involved.

The various issues treated here interact in a number of ways, and the appropriate icons are displayed to allow cross-referencing between factsheets.

2. Glossary

The glossary provides explanations of the various environmental concepts referred to in this work, as well as basic definitions in current use.

It refers, via icons, to the issue-based factsheets.

3. Bibliography

This refers to the principal sources which were used as reference material by the editorial team preparing this report.

Please consult the bibliography for other bibliographical sources for further reading.

4. Timeline

It is of benefit to every user of this work to be able to visualise how environmental issues, and their management, have developed over time. The timeline illustrates this in the light of certain events, political decisions and the measures implemented.

The key dates given on this timeline identify four major types of events and actions:

- world events;
- the evolution of the European Union;
- ecological disasters; and
- Europe's environmental action.

Here, too, the use of icons allows the reader to refer quickly to those issue-based factsheets which are particularly closely linked to these events.

5. Using the work

There are three ways of accessing information on a particular issue:

- through the central document, with its issue-based factsheets;
- through the timeline; or
- through the glossary.

The reader chooses direct access to the factsheets through the central document

The reader chooses the factsheet dealing with the issue in which he or she is most interested. The reader then has access to a body of information on the chosen topic. More in-depth research may be carried out by referring to other issues via the icons.

The reader chooses to refer to the timeline

The reader consults the important key dates relating to the topic in which he or she is interested. Icons are then used to refer the reader to the issue-based factsheets in the central document.

The reader chooses an entry on the topic in which he/she is interested

From here, the reader selects the words and key concepts relating to the topic in which he or she is interested.

Using icons, these concepts then refer the reader to the issue-based factsheets in the central document.

The problems caused by global economic development have grown increasingly acute over the past 20 years. Although a lot of progress has been made in certain areas, the environmental warning-lights continue to flash. Europe has a special part to play in the ecological context, given its status as a highly industrialised and developed region, and the European Union takes its responsibilities very seriously. EU environmental policy has already achieved some beneficial results, but a lot more development is still needed in this field.

The single most important shift that has occurred over the past 20 years is the fact that environmental protection has now become an inseparable part of economic development. Slowly but surely, European and even global environmental programmes are giving our small blue planet a new chance. Protecting the environment certainly requires our political leaders to take action, but the everyday choices of each and every one of us can be no less important. We will begin with a review of the current state of the environment.

For the generation to come

1970s - environmentalism comes of age

Environmental awareness has grown steadily since the 1970s. The primary goals at first were simply to contain environmental problems, reduce health risks, regulate planning and development and protect threatened species and habitats, all in the short term. The main feature of the first generation of policies (1970-85) was their highly sectoral approach towards the environment and the actions to be taken (air, water, waste and so on tended to be viewed in isolation). The spotlight fell mainly on the battle against pollution and resources remained relatively limited.

1980s - thinking globally

A substantial shift has occurred since the late 1980s. Early environmental action turned out to have little visible effect and damage continued to be inflicted in a number of areas. What's more, in addition to local problems, evidence emerged of environmental damage

Sunset, Renney Rocks near Plymouth (U.K.).
Source : Spectrum Colour Library.

on a global scale, such as climate change and the depletion of the ozone layer. Some products were found to pollute geographical areas far away from where they were emitted. Not even the polar ice caps have been spared. Finally, long-term, cumulative effects have been discovered that could pose a significant threat to future generations.

Economic challenge

Having once been seen as contrary to business interests, environmentalism has steadily become an important element of the industrial system, with a growing influence on technology and products. The environment has become an increasingly significant factor shaping corporate strategy. What's more, environmental technologies and products have themselves become a growth sector which is spearheading innovation and creating employment.

The idea of sustainable development

Brundtland Report

UNCED, the United Nations Commission on the Environment and Development, clearly established in 1987 that the environment was deteriorating steadily and that this was directly linked to regional and global economic development. The commission published its findings as the 'Brundtland Report', which also warned that some forms of environmental damage (climate change and hazardous wastes, for instance) were being passed on systematically to future generations. The report showed the world that environmental problems cannot be separated from issues of human welfare and general economic development.

Alternative development

The Brundtland Report argued in favour of alternative forms of development that could ensure economic growth in both the short and long term while simultaneously improving the environment and preserving natural resources. Development of this kind has been christened 'sustainability' - the only way to avert economic or ecological catastrophe in the medium to long run. Sustainable development must be capable of 'meeting current needs without compromising the ability of future generations to meet theirs'. The notion of sustainability marks a turning point in economic and environmental policy-making and has been widely accepted and approved.

Prevention and restoration

The fact that sustainable development is believed to be compatible with economic growth has undoubtedly contributed to this acceptance. Stronger than that, a growing economy is actually seen as a necessary precondition for sustainability, in that it creates the resources needed for ecological development, the restoration of earlier environmental damage and the prevention of future harm.

Changing models of growth

We are faced with the challenge of modifying our familiar models of economic growth. Every citizen has to understand that the quality and preservation of the natural environment and its resources are vital to continued social and economic development. As part of this process, we have to stop seeing economic growth as an end in itself but as a factor that can help improve the quality of our living environment.

Rio Conference

Integration

The UN Conference on Environment and Development held in Rio in June 1992 focused on the need to incorporate the idea of sustainable development into environmental and economic policy-making. The international community gathered at Rio accepted (albeit in a very general way) the aim of sustainable development for the whole world.

Agenda 21

The concrete results of the Rio Conference were as follows.

The Rio Declaration on Environment and Development. The aim here is to work towards sustainable development, to eliminate non-viable modes of production and consumption and to establish a global partnership in this field.

The Climate Change Convention sets the objective of stabilising greenhouse gas concentrations at a level that does not threaten the world's climate. This is to be done by setting up national and regional programmes and strategies. The convention also sets the target of stabilising emissions of CO_2 (the most significant greenhouse gas) by the year 2000.

The Biodiversity Convention aims to safeguard the variety of species and ecosystems.

The Forest Declaration acknowledges the vital role forests play in nurturing ecosystems, water resources, climate and biological diversity. It organises the introduction of protective measures and calls on nations, consumers and producers of tropical hardwoods to use forests in the most sustainable way possible.

Agenda 21, finally, is a general plan integrating all the actions to be taken by the international community in all fields relating to sustainable development through to the 21st century.

Commitment

Signatories to the Rio agreements have agreed to draw up plans for implementing the various conventions and declarations. The first draft of Agenda 21 runs to 800 pages and 40 chapters, which set out a planetary protection programme costing $ 600 billion for 180 individual states at different stages of ecological development and awareness. It will be a challenge, to say the least.

Rio + 5, Rio + 0?

In June 1997, the 160 Rio signatories met for a second Earth Summit in New York. Although some encouraging results had been obtained since Rio, the final conference document expressed profound concern at the accelerating deterioration of the environment and participants had to acknowledge that the overall outlook had grown more sombre.

Far from diminishing, for instance, greenhouse gas emissions have continued to grow. The battle against desertification, the need to protect biodiversity and several other urgent concerns were reaffirmed, but no extra funds were pledged. The systematic application of Agenda 21 remains vitally important, but has yet to begin on a significant scale. For its part, the European Union has proposed that all industrialised countries reduce their CO_2 emissions to 85% of 1990 levels by 2010. We can only hope that Japan and the United States will come on board by 1999 when the next international conference on climate is scheduled.

The European Union's Fifth Environment Programme

European environmental action takes the form of five-year action programmes.
The first four European environment programmes (1973-1992) led to the introduction of over 200 legislative measures. The Fifth Programme, adopted towards the end of 1992, marked a fundamental new approach.

From the Maastricht Treaty...

The Maastricht Treaty, signed in February 1992, gave the environment a more prominent place in the policies of the European Community and its member states. The treaty sets out to:
- Promote sustainable and environmentally friendly development;
- Establish a high level of environmental protection;
- Integrate environmental needs in policy-making and implementation in other sectors.

From now on, therefore, sustainable development will be one of the main objectives of the European project.

... to the Fifth Environment Programme.

The European Community's Fifth Environment Programme

Summary of programme in certain target sectors

	SECTORAL IMPACT	RESOURCES	ACTIONS
INDUSTRY	Integrated tackling of pollution	Reduction and enhanced management of waste	Eco-labelling of products
ENERGY	Reducing pollution	Development of renewable resources	Reducing energy consumption
TRANSPORT	More environment-friendly vehicles and fuels	Rationalisation of infrastructure	Improved car management
AGRICULTURE	Ecologically sustainable farming	Development of forests	Rural development
TOURISM	Sustainable tourism - Town and country planning - Infrastructure	Protection of coastal zones and natural assets	Increased choice and better seasonal distribution.

'Towards Sustainability' covers the period 1993-2000. It sets out an overall strategy leading progressively towards sustainable development and defines five sectors in which the environment ought to have more influence on policy and where significant action is required.

Fields, objectives and targets

For each sector (industry, energy, transport, agriculture and tourism) there are established objectives, targets and timetables.

Shared responsibility

This strategy also addresses the responsibility of the key players (government, companies, local communities and the public) because progress can only be made if everyone recognises the importance of the work to be done and their own part in it.

A challenge for Europe

Urgent changes

Future generations have just as much right to clean air, pure water and green forests as we do, but that right is currently under severe threat. We have all become aware of the danger posed to the environment by the uncontrolled exploitation of the earth's natural resources. The greenhouse effect, the depletion of the earth's protective ozone layer and the systematic destruction of tropical rainforests are only three examples of how the limits of sustainability have been breached. After two decades of what was essentially corrective action (and not always successful at that), the Community now prefers to emphasise partnership and shared responsibility when it comes to preventing and, if possible, reversing environmental damage.

Europe's response

The European Union has adopted over 200 directives since 1970 with the aim of improving air and water quality, controlling waste disposal, monitoring industrial risks and protecting nature. Key aims of this legislation have been to restrict sul-

Education. Source : Mike St Maur Sheil

Advances in environmental protection as measured by progress towards achieving Fifth Programme targets (index 1985 = 100)

	1985	1990	Target for year 2000	Likelihood of meeting target
GLOBAL SCALE				
CO_2 emissions	100 (1)	102	102	+/-
CFC production	100 (2)	64	0 (3)	+
EUROPEAN SCALE				
SO_2 emissions	100 (1)	88	65	+
NO_x emissions	100 (1)	107	70	-
VOC emissions	100	101	70 (4)	-
REGIONAL SCALE				
Per capita urban waste	100	115	100	-
Noise > 65 dB	100	>100	100	+/-
Pesticides in groundwater	100	>100	0 (5)	-
Nitrates in groundwater	100	>100	0	-

NB : + target will probably be met
+/- uncertain
- unlikely

(1) Including the former East Germany, (2) In 1986, (3) By 1995, (4) By 1999, (5) By 2005

Source : European Environment Agency.

phur emissions (the primary cause of acid rain), ban the use of products that harm the ozone layer, control transport, eliminate hazardous waste and establish safety standards for bathing waters at all EU beaches. This approach culminated in the adoption of the Fifth Programme shortly after the Rio Conference.

In addition to traditional legislative actions, the European Union wishes to use a broad spectrum of tools in order to achieve a sustainable society:

- Economic instruments, to encourage good products and processes.
- Financial instruments, of which LIFE is the only one directly dedicated to the environment.

Since its inception in 1992, it has co-financed over one thousand demonstration projects for industry and local authorities and nature protection actions. The Commission also works closely together with the Member States to add an environmental dimension to the Community Funds.

- Support measures (information, education, research).

Interim review

Mixed results

The Commission drew up an interim review of its progress in 1996. Progress has been made in integration of environmental considerations into other policy areas. Progress is most advanced in the manufacturing sector where legislation has existed for twenty years and where the economic advantages were quickly seen, and it is least apparent in agriculture and in tourism. In the field of transport, awareness of the problems is increasing, progress is being made on vehicle emissions, fuel quality and technology, but the overall growth in the number of vehicles negates progress. In the energy sector,

although the environment is seen as part of the problem and of the solution, there is a lack of internalisation of environmental costs into the price of energy.

In a number of sectors, the evolution of the quality of the environment is emphasised in the report of the European Environment Agency : on chlorofluorocarbons (CFCs), halons, nitrogen oxides (NOx), volatile organic compounds (VOCs) and heavy metals.

In some other sectors, possible improvements are awaited by the year 2000 :

- Sulphur dioxide emissions (SO_2);
- Production of ozone-depleting substances;
- Heavy metal discharges into the North Sea via the atmosphere and continental waters;
- Carbon dioxide (CO_2) emissions. Despite considerable uncertainty, reductions by the year 2000 may be seen as a first step towards future reductions.

Could do better

The EU is on the right path in some areas but it is still far from sure of meeting its objectives in the following sectors:

- Acidification. The widespread breaching of critical limits will continue;
- Volatile organic compounds (VOCs). There has been a clear reduction in VOC emissions, but the slow implementation of directives makes it unlikely that targets will be met by the year 2000;
- Nitrates. Drinking water standards will be breached less frequently thanks to substantial reductions in the use of nitrogen in farming, but the persistence of nitrates in groundwater is such that the targets will not be met without denitrification;
- Waste management. Waste generation continues to grow steadily, despite waste prevention policies. Future gains from recycling will be undermined

by the expense of the procedures and the lack of markets for recycled materials;

- The urban environment. Pressures in this area, especially those linked to traffic, will continue to worsen in most cities;
- Conserving and protecting biodiversity. The pressure exerted by transport and tourism continues to intensify, even though a growing number of areas are protected and agricultural problems are diminishing in response to changes in the CAP (Common Agricultural Policy) and ecological farming measures.

Achieving aims

In order to achieve the Fifth Programme objectives, the Commission adopted a Proposal for a decision on an Action Plan for a better implementation of this Programme, which stresses five priorities :

- better integration of the environment into other policies.
- use of a broader range of instruments.
- increased implementation of legislation.
- better information and communication.
- international leadership.

Groves landscape : Source : Mike St Maur Sheil

WHAT CAN YOU DO?
THE CITIZEN'S ROLE

Citizens are environmental players, too.

There are several things we can do to safeguard the future of humanity and that of the earth by acting locally. We can join an environmental organisation, carefully consider the daily choices we make as consumers ('green consumption') and get involved as citizens and voters in regional development projects.

Sustainable development isn't just an abstract notion to be left to our political leaders. In reality, the environment can only be protected by actions that are often simple but highly effective when repeated by thousands if not millions of consumers. To help you take concrete action, we have created a room-by-room tour of the average house, focusing on the relevant themes in each one. Although we can't offer a comprehensive guide to ecologically sound living, once you start thinking about these things, you'll soon find you're able to come up with appropriate ecological behaviour for a wide range of family or working situations.

We admit, however, that although greener living can sometimes save us money (lower fuel bills, for instance) it can also require substantial investment (installing a rainwater tank, choosing more expensive 'green' products, etc.). Protecting the environment and our health comes with a price tag that none us can afford to dodge.

Living room

You may be reading this in your armchair in the living room, wondering how to translate the rather abstract notion of sustainable development into everyday terms. We might as well begin with the light you need to read these pages. The first thing we do when the sun goes down is to turn on a light. We have as much domestic energy as we want nowadays and it is only on the rare occasion of a power cut that we suddenly realise how dependent we have become on electricity.

To reduce consumption, you could switch to fluorescent or other energy-saving bulbs, which use only a quarter of the energy to generate the same amount of light and last up to ten times longer. Apart from the direct economic benefit, switching bulbs in this way also helps protect the environment. The power we consume is relatively cheap because the price we pay does not reflect the true environmental costs of generating electricity (consumption of non-renewable fossil fuels, disposing of nuclear waste, etc.). Domestic energy consumption is growing steadily as new labour-saving appliances continue to make our lives easier.

You can, however, stabilise and even reduce your electricity consumption via a few simple actions. Adjust lighting to your actual needs (e.g. by installing neon tubes in the garage and kitchen), choose appliances with lower energy consumption, turn out the lights when you leave a room and use direct rather than indirect lighting. You can also keep an eye on off-peak consumption - energy may cost less at night, but its environmental impact is just the same.

Kitchen

The kitchen has got to be one of the most frequently visited and liveliest rooms in any house. It's here, of course, that meals are prepared and often eaten. The kitchen is very much a strategic room - a place of communication and discussion and a food store. It is also here that we keep our main domestic appliances (fridge, dishwasher, mixer, coffee-maker, kettle, microwave, etc.) and wash and dry our dishes. Every one of these activities has environmental implications in terms of energy conservation, saving water and ecologically aware consumption.

The kitchen is also the place where waste management begins. In an attempt to tackle the growing volume of domestic waste, many local communities organise the selective collection of paper, cardboard, glass, metals and minor chemical waste. Some encourage the composting of organic waste, as home-made compost improves soil quality while reducing the volume of domestic refuse by around 40%.

In many cases, therefore, people's kitchens have become mini-sorting centres. We should clearly understand, however, that sorting and recycling waste is a responsibility taken on in perpetuity. One effect of managing your own household waste is to make you realise that the best kind of waste is the kind you don't produce in the first place. Watch out for excessive packaging at the time of purchase, give preference to durable and non-polluting products and buy correct amounts to avoid waste. In short, we all need to apply the principle of prevention.

Bathroom

Have you ever wondered, during your morning or evening ablutions, how much water you consume every day in keeping yourself clean? Washing your hands uses anywhere between 2 and 18 litres, brushing your teeth 0.2 to 5 litres and taking a bath 150 to 200 litres. Not to mention those seemingly insignificant little leaks. A dripping tap can waste 35 cubic metres of water a year and a toilet with an incorrectly adjusted flush as much as 220 cubic metres! Carelessness like this can cost a lot when your water's metered, to say nothing of the environmental impact. What's more, the water in question is usually drinking water. We're used to having unlimited amounts of good-quality water on tap at a ridiculously low price, blinding us to the fact that drinking water is a precious and rare resource that needs to be conserved.

Away from the bathroom, we can always use alternative water supplies like rainwater for a variety of purposes - cleaning the house, watering the plants or filling the washing machine or toilet. Another habit to be avoided is disinfecting toilets with bleach. It isn't effective and is very harmful to health and the environment, as bleach contains chlorine which reacts with organic compounds in water to form dangerous and persistent organochlorines (mutagens, carcinogens, etc.) which can then build up in the food chain.

Bedroom

The bedroom is a very important part of the home in which we spend many hours every day. It is a room that deserves a lot of attention, from noise levels to lighting, heating and furnishings and, most important of all, air quality. Bedrooms should be well ventilated and should not have fitted carpets, as these can cause allergies. Certain materials used in construction, decoration and furniture can also emit substances that are harmful to health and the environment over a prolonged period. It's always best to use natural materials like stone, wood, cork, natural plaster and cotton and to choose paints and other products that are water rather than solvent-based. You can use dried flowers, spices and fruit to perfume rooms and wardrobes, rather than spraying chemical air-fresheners. As for cleaning, finally, the best solution is light and regular washing with an environmentally friendly detergent.

Garage

Garages are often workshops in which cars cohabit with bikes and scooters, gardening tools, lawn-mowers, tool-boxes and workbenches. Many of them have shelves filled with products of varying age, from bottles of distilled water to paints, pesticides and highly-toxic solvents. You should always follow the storage instructions for these products, make sure that the label is properly legible and that the use-by date hasn't lapsed. They should be kept away from heat and damp, and most important of all, out of reach of children. If you need to get rid of any of these products, you should never just throw them into the dustbin or pour them down the drain or onto the ground, as they are far too harmful to the environment and human health (they can give off toxic gases, for instance). Contact your local waste-collection service to find out what you should do with household chemical waste.

Talking about garages naturally brings us to the car. Car-use should be taken into account when choosing somewhere to live. The ideal home has a garden, even a small one, and a garage for your bikes, and should be close to work, public transport connections and shopping facilities. You can then use your car in combination with public transport, walking and cycling, something which children particularly enjoy. The environmental impact of cars is focused on elsewhere in this book. Suffice it to say that our cities are literally suffocating under the effects of car use, yet this is only one aspect of the overall problem.

Garden

The garden is a place of relaxation for the whole family. Many gardens are far from perfect, acting as home to weeds and slugs which try to beat us to the lettuce. The ideal garden for a lot of people would be totally free of weeds, pests and disease and should have plenty of flowers. Modern gardeners can achieve this ideal without many hours of work by turning to a whole arsenal of chemical products, from artificial fertilisers to pesticides, none of which are entirely free of health and environmental side-effects. We can, however, enjoy productive and healthy gardens without resorting to chemical products. If we make our own compost we can fertilise our soil cheaply and effectively, while substantially reducing the volume of our household refuse. We can have our soil analysed to see whether we need to increase the amount of nutrients. We can also use living organisms or their products to deal with any pests that take a fancy to our plants. Ladybirds, for instance, are great greenfly predators.

Judicious combination and rotation of plant species, finally, can also significantly improve the quality of our gardens.

Changing the world

We live in a society that pushes us to consume more and more all the time. Manufacturers and service-providers are constantly encouraging us to buy. Attitudes towards cars reveal a lot about a society. For the average citizen, the car is a symbol of social success. The newer, more attractive, comfortable and powerful the car, the higher its owner has climbed the social ladder. At least that's what many consumers believe. The number of cars per household is another supposed indicator of social success. Meanwhile, cars are becoming increasingly recyclable, fitted with catalytic converters and thrifty in fuel consumption, all of which eases the consumer's conscience and pushes public and alternative forms of transport into the background. Immense financial interests are at stake, not to mention jobs - directly in the case of car design, construction, distribution and maintenance and indirectly for the road, healthcare and insurance industries. As time goes by, however, we are having to pay a mounting environmental cost as the air becomes unbreathable in our cities. And the lives of many citizens have been left miserable and dangerous by the car. How, for instance, can we increase road safety around our schools when it has become the norm to drive our kids directly to the school gate? In many areas, no-one in their right mind would let their children cycle to school any more. The environmental revolution we need can only happen if there is a real change in mentality. Only then will the idea of sustainability be truly enshrined in our daily lives. We mustn't leave it too late to act.

Facts and Trends
The pressure of humanity

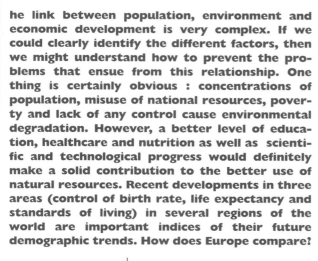

he link between population, environment and economic development is very complex. If we could clearly identify the different factors, then we might understand how to prevent the problems that ensue from this relationship. One thing is certainly obvious : concentrations of population, misuse of national resources, poverty and lack of any control cause environmental degradation. However, a better level of education, healthcare and nutrition as well as scientific and technological progress would definitely make a solid contribution to the better use of natural resources. Recent developments in three areas (control of birth rate, life expectancy and standards of living) in several regions of the world are important indices of their future demographic trends. How does Europe compare?

Austria, Finland and Sweden recently joined the European Union, which had hitherto been one of the most densely populated areas in the world with 147 inhabitants per km2. The addition of the immense Scandinavian territories (27% of the EU's surface area with only 6% of its total population) reduced this figure to 114 inhabitants per km². The distribution of the EU's population is, however, extremely unequal. The density in Finland is a mere 15 inhabitants/km², rising to 331 in Belgium and 372 in the Netherlands. Some 20% of Europe's 370 million citizens live within 4% of its territory, primarily in the highly urbanised industrial areas and along the coasts. This has inevitably created a concentrated release of pollutants into the environment and has led to the development of all related infrastructures and networks in society : transport, telecommunications, electricity etc.

One important response to these problems lies in the approach we take to planning and how we use the land. We can see this in the Netherlands for example which has the densest population in Europe whilst enjoying vast areas of green belt and open spaces.

Well informed and more aware, Europe's citizens, as consumers, can make more responsible and better informed choices which can reduce the pressure on our environment.

Profile

Higher standards of living is the fundamental cause for the growth of material consumption in Europe which has grown spectacularly in the last 40 years. A second factor has been the overall growth of population in that period, some 17% since 1964 despite a levelling off of the birth rate in recent years. The average European also lives longer (to an average age of 72 for men and 79 for women). As the number of pensioners has rapidly increased so has the desire to travel. Retired people have plenty of free time and in many cases are better off financially than their juniors. This makes them important consumers of leisure services and holidays. The sharp increase in European consumption of goods and services can also be attributed to other factors, including shrinking average households (more people living alone).

Struggling to keep up

Europe actually stands out from the rest of the world for its lack of demographic dynamism. In 1993, net population growth in the EU ranged from 5 for every 1,000 inhabitants in Ireland to -1.2 in Germany. The recent collapse in the birthrate in Spain, Greece, the Netherlands and Ireland will further accelerate the relative ageing of the population in those regions.

2 out of 3 citizens are town-dwellers

Recent decades have seen the closure of many farms and the loss of 2 million jobs in rural areas. This has significantly altered the pattern of population distribution. The amount of land under cultivation has declined steadily in Europe since the beginning of the 1960s. Conversely, reforestation and natural tree growth led to a 10% increase in forested area over the same period. Virgin land or properties abandoned by bankrupt farmers and rural workers drawn to the city have often been bought up and used to build new homes and businesses, infrastructure or recreational facilities. The growing imbalance between town and countryside has led to increased consumption of energy and transport. It has been calculated that the combined effect of urbanisation and mobility in Europe's most densely populated countries causes built-up areas to increase by 2% every 10 years. According to these findings, the road network is eating up an additional 1.3% of Europe's total land area every year compared to a mere 0.03% in the case of rail.

Europe in action
New approaches

Source : Eurostat

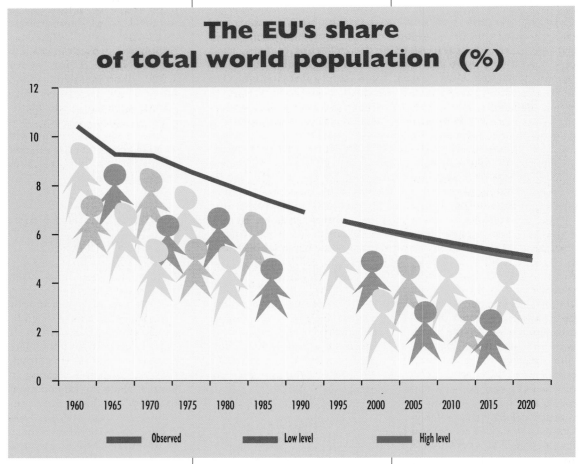

The EU's share of total world population (%)

Observed — Low level — High level

Europe's industrial landscape has changed a great deal over the past 20 years. Heavy industry has declined (a process that began somewhat later in the East) and the service and high technology sectors have increased in growth tremendously. These changes, together with measures taken in the field of energy efficiency have helped the EU make important progress over the past 20 years in terms of the efficiency of energy consumption.

Everything we produce and consume has an impact on the environment. Above all, it is the way goods are produced that decides how big this impact will be. The explosive increase in oil prices in the early 1970s, growing environmental awareness

Housing in the Isle of Dogs, London, UK. Source : Spectrum colour Library.

and the introduction of the first environmental regulations forced Europe to restructure economically. Technological advances have also occurred in the three main fields of energy-saving, material substitution and pollution control. This is clearly apparent when we review the pattern of industry's energy and raw material consumption in recent decades (the rate of energy use measured in terms of gross domestic consumption per unit of GDP has been reduced by 25%). A similar picture appears through the explosion of new businesses working in the field of environmental protection. What's more, the breakthrough of information society technologies could ensure better management of natural resources and more effective pollution control in the future.

No doubt that by the end of the 1990s, all the most effective steps in this field will already have been taken. In other words, if the European economy and population continue to grow at the present rate, the measures we will have to introduce in the future to maintain or reduce current emission rates will be increasingly complex and onerous. For that reason it is important we act quickly.

Managing our land more effectively

The EU has redoubled its efforts to support effective and more integrated town and regional planning policy. It is well known that

simply providing structural funds is no longer enough, nor completely efficient, especially as the results of such investments can be environmentally damaging. The current priority is to sketch the outlines of Europe's future expansion, part of which entails implementing the Europe 2000+ report (1994) which laid the foundations for co-operation in the field of European land

development. The report places particular stress on the need to protect the environment, safeguard biodiversity and manage natural resources prudently. It also emphasises the need for cross-border, inter-regional and transnational co-operation within the EU itself and with neighbouring countries if we are to achieve our shared objective of promoting sustainable development.

A drop in the birth-rate shows up as a reduction at the base of the pyramid. At the same time, however, the apex is rising because people are living longer. What we see here is two processes acting at the same time.

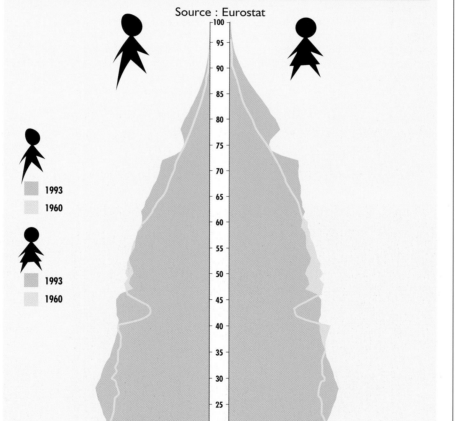

Demographic pyramid in the EU : comparison between 1960/1993 (% of world population).

Source : Eurostat

1993
1960

1993
1960

Taking responsibility

PRIORITY OBJECTIVES

- Introduce measures to improve energy efficiency.
- Enhance processes and technology.
- Improve pollution control.
- Reduce emissions and discharges.
- **Introduce environmental management tools (LCA).**

The impact of development

The quality of the environment and the growing concentration of population is a clear challenge for our societies. Simply defining these two factors more effectively would go a long way towards a cleaver picture of a more symbiotic relationship between our civilisation and nature.

Town and country planning is frequently used as an instrument for protecting the environment. Plans can be drawn up at national or regional level, but the system generally operates at local level. Some states use sector plans incorporating specific ecological objectives, such as programmes for restoring environmental damage in eastern Germany, land-use plans for coastal zones in Portugal, regional plans for discharge points in the Netherlands and plans for integrated transport management in Austria. The public is increasingly involved in the drafting of these plans - a factor that has been the norm in recent years for Northern Europe and which is now also spreading to the countries of the South, as demonstrated by Portugal's recent national environment plan.

Physical planning has to be seen as one aspect of an overall strategy of environmental policy.

Soaring growth rates

The impact of demographic and economic growth on the well-being of our planet has been measured in the following terms:

- Tripling of the population over the last 100 years and a doubling in the last 40;
- 20-fold increase in economic activity;
- 50-fold increase in the consumption of fossil fuels;
- 50-fold increase in industrial output.

Denmark, France, Ireland, Norway, the Netherlands and the UK have all risen to the challenge, drafting Green Plans for the year 2000. The basic idea in each case is to address environmental problems at their source, taking them directly into account when formulating national policy and the codes of conduct to be pursued by the various sectors of business.

Tourism in Amsterdam
Source : Benelux Press.

INDUSTRIAL ACTIVITY

TRANSPORT

ENERGY

Facts and Trends
Greening industry

ndustry is an immense source of wealth and comfort for modern society, but it is also responsible for much pollution that threatens our health and environment. There is an urgent need nowadays to add an ecological dimension to economic development and to reconcile competition with respect for the environment. Although this is an immense challenge, it is one that can and must be met.

Portrait

The EU's annual industrial output is worth around ECU 2,600 billion, putting it alongside the United States and Japan as one of the world's leading industrial powers. European manufacturing is currently growing at a rate of 2% a year, compared to a 1993 forecast of 2.6% annual growth until the year 2000. Some 80% of the industrial sector is made up of small and medium-sized firms and it is directly responsible for around 25% of Europe's wealth.

Environment alert

By definition, all industrial activity uses up natural resources, consumes energy, generates waste and releases pollution. If the environment is not to be damaged irreversibly, it is crucial that we continue to reduce this damage at a rapid pace. Current levels are downright alarming (see table). What's more, our raw materials are running out.

Production up, pollution down

Recent technological advances, the decline of heavy industry and the growth of the service sector have helped reduce consumption per unit produced of energy and raw materials significantly. In many cases, however, these advances have been accompanied by increased production. In the chemical industry, for instance, unit energy consumption fell 30% between 1980 and 1989, but production rose 50% over the same period.

Cleaner technology

Prior to the 1980s, virtually no account was taken of environmental concerns when it came to shaping industrial processes. Stricter environmental legislation and demand on the part of consumers for greener products are, however, obliging industrial companies to take more and more notice of the environment in their business plans. This is best illustrated by the development of 'clean technology' throughout industry. The purpose of such technology is to **prevent** pollution rather than **curing** it. It means that fewer raw materials are used to manufacture the same finished product and that less pollution is generated in the process.

Industry's contribution to the main environmental issues (1995, list not exhaustive)

ENVIRONMENTAL ISSUE	INDUSTRY'S SHARE	
• Climate change	• 27 %	of CO_2 emissions
	24 %	of N_2O emissions
• Destruction of the ozone layer	• 80 %	of CFC emissions
• Acidification of the environment	• 29 %	of SO_2 emissions,
	13 %	of NO_x emissions
• Air pollution	• 30 %	of VOC emissions
• Waste materials	• 29 %	of waste production
• Water resources	• 53 %	of water consumption
	7 %	of phosphorous discharges
	10 %	of nitrogen discharges
• Urban environment	• 10 %	of noise emissions

Europe in action

Environment and competitiveness

It was once widely believed that economic development was incompatible with ecological concerns. Nowadays, it has become clear that we both can and must create and recreate industries that are compatible with the protection of the environment. European policy sets out to encourage ecologically friendly production, stressing that 'as far as the environment is concerned, industry is not only part of the problem, it is also one of the keys to its solution'.

Objectives

Europe's strategic goal is for ecological concerns to be steadily integrated in industrial policy. In 1993, the European Commission published a White Paper on 'Growth, competitiveness and employment', in which it argued that if Europe was to prosper economically while simultaneously reducing pollution, it would have to:

- Perfect manufacturing techniques capable of reducing consumption of raw materials and the generation of pollution;
- Extend the useful life of products;
- Establish reuse and recycling as the norm;
- Develop more reliable products.

Measures

A collection of measures and support instruments have been adopted in this regard. Whilst fiscal and financial incentives like eco-taxes are considered important they have proven difficult in practice (for example the CO_2/energy tax project - see 'Climate'). Therefore, a number of important new requirements have also been introduced on a purely legislative level, including:

- Regulations for **chemical products** which set out packaging, labelling, transport and marketing standards for all hazardous substances .
- A directive on **major accident risks** associated with certain industrial activities ('Seveso' Directive).
- A **system for assessing the environmental impact** of certain public or private projects. Permission to go ahead with these projects is now based on a compulsory environmental impact assessment. The latter is available to the public who can submit opinions which must be taken into account by the regulating authority when deciding whether or not to grant permission for the project.
- Rules to reward environmentally friendly products by allowing them to display an **eco-label**.
- An **eco-management and audit system** to encourage firms to evaluate and steadily improve their environmental performance, in return for use of the 'EMAS' logo and an

Cleansing contaminated soil, Holland.Source : Michael St Maur Sheil.

enhanced brand image ('EMAS' regulation).

- A directive on **packaging** setting out recycling standards for waste packaging.
- A directive on **integrated pollution prevention and control,** which introduces a new approach to emission prevention through the control of pollution from air, water and soil in large industrial and agricultural installations. The Directive replaces the old 'end-of-pipe' solution which tried to control final discharges with an approach which uses technology to minimise emissions at every stage of the industrial process. ('IPPC' Directive).

Results

Despite some pollution prevention and the conservation of natural resources (especially water) have yet to be adequately integrated in either industrial policy or practice. Important progress has been achieved where the following conditions apply:

- The source of the pollution is well defined;
- Anti-pollution techniques are available at the beginning of the chain;

Developments

The Good...   ...the Bad

- New economic instruments that encourage industry to add an environmental dimension to their production and management policies.
- Development of less polluting processes and products.
- The availability of relatively inexpensive technical solutions for reducing certain types of pollution;
- Improved management and control of production processes.
- The closure of heavy industries and the development of the service sector (which is less voracious in its consumption of raw materials and energy).
- Growth in production and consumption.
- Increasing demand for energy (despite improved energy efficiency in some industrial processes).
- The low price of certain products (especially fossil fuels), which discourages real savings.
- The cost of introducing clean technology.

- The measures in question only entail a low level of costs (improving energy efficiency, for instance, or reducing waste).

Progress in other fields, however, has been **very modest or inadequate:**
- Controlling emissions;
- Developing clean technology;
- Reducing packaging waste;
- Integrated pollution prevention.

The growing cost of caring for the environment

It has been calculated that by the year 2000, industry will have taken most of the measures that require only a relatively modest investment. Consequently, as economic and demographic growth continue, the measures needed to keep emissions at or below current levels will become increasingly complex and onerous.

Lorraine, France
Source : Benelux Press

Taking responsibility

Member state level

Member States can, with EU support, promote 'eco-industries' and encourage traditional industry to make a 'green breakthrough'. This entails the following measures (some countries have, of course, already begun to act in this field):

- Improving the spread of clean technology and promoting ecological best practice;
- Stressing the benefits of a positive attitude towards environmental problems;
- Launching support programmes for SMEs to encourage them to switch to less polluting technologies by means of practical and financial assistance;
- Providing information and raising awareness to encourage changes in consumer behaviour.

As far as preventing industrial pollution is concerned, the directive on environmental impact assessments has proved very effective and is now beginning to bear fruit.

Big business quicker to respond

Industrial companies wishing to reduce their environmental costs and improve their brand image have been steadily incorporating environmental concerns in their business plans. For many of them, a more environmentally friendly approach has become an important marketing tool. Some have signed 'sustainable development charters', while others have opted for voluntary codes drawn up by Europe, such as the eco-label and eco-audit (EMAS) schemes. Others still have signed voluntary agreements with their respective governments, committing themselves to go further than existing standards require. Many industries have also turned towards the concept of eco-efficiency and the opportunity offered by technology to reduce inputs and power consumption in the production process. This has a dual effect, lower costs and better competitiveness for industry and less waste and lower emissions for our environment.

What about SMEs?

It is at the level of small and medium-sized enterprises that progress towards greater environmental protection has been weakest, in spite of the fact that both the EU and individual Member States provide expert technical and financial assistance to support SMEs in their environmental efforts. Because of their size, companies in this category ought to be flexible and adaptable, giving them a potential advantage in certain new and existing markets (environmental services, product recycling, etc.). Their development is often held back, however, by restrictive administrative, financial or legal requirements.

The citizen's role

Europe's citizens can play an important part in persuading industry to take fuller account of the environment. They can support cleaner companies by preferring ecologically friendly products (phosphate-free washing powder, CFC-free aerosols, recycled paper, reusable products, etc.). Citizens can also urge industrial firms to take part in the European eco-management and audit system (EMAS) or to sign an environmental charter.

Environmental impact assessments, meanwhile, offer local residents greater involvement in the authorising or rejection of certain categories of public or private project.

HISTORICAL ENVIRONMENTAL MANAGEMENT TRENDS.

	Pre-1970s	1970s–80s	1990s
	Few regulations/ limited focus – air/water	Compliance/ reactive	Prevention/ proactive
General approach	Hazardous waste not an issue	'End-of-pipe' control	Life-cycle approach
Management			Environmental audit
Organisational structure	Limited corporate environmental presence	Corporate environmental presence functionally isolated	Full environmental integration throughout business
Costs	Environmental costs low	Environment is a cost to be minimised	The environment is a strategic opportunity to be seized

Source : ERM.

Facts and Trends
The earth's clogged arteries

Transport is growing at an unprecedented rate. Not only does it consume immense quantities of energy and space, it has also been identified as one of the main sources of atmospheric and noise pollution. Most worrying of all, road traffic, the most damaging form of transport, is also the most popular.

There has been an explosion in freight and passenger traffic in recent decades as the economy has grown and people have become increasingly mobile (work and leisure travel). The number of kilometres travelled by the average road user rose by 40% between 1980 and 1990.

To meet this demand, governments have increased the number of building works for network infrastructures. They have stepped up their road-construction programmes (to meet demand for the most popular form of transport) and have built numerous airports and high-speed rail links.

These measures have had to be taken, however, against a background of intense competition, which has tended to outweigh the necessary balance and integration between the different modes of transport. From the environmental point of view, traffic growth is very worrying. Transport accounts for 25% of total CO_2 emissions in Europe and is a major source of noise pollution, up to 80% of the total nuisance in some countries. As it expands, it inevitably increases the burden placed on the environment. From congestion and the threat of gridlock to network maintenance, accidents and respiratory complaints, the social costs of our much-prized mobility are self evident.

Cities under threat

It is hardly surprising then that an increase in traffic growth has all but cancelled out the impact of technological advances such as the introduction of catalytic converters and other improvements. City dwellers are becoming increasingly resentful of the damage to health caused by poor air quality, which is largely the result of vehicle emissions. New European air quality standards will oblige cities to review their transport policies and to find new ways of providing citizens with access to work, recreation and cultural activities, while simultaneously protecting their quality of life. Cities in Europe which have already introduced this new approach are encouraged to exchange their respective experiences. It also has to recognise that external factors like price, quality and variety of service, journey length and the organisation of social and economic life will continue to influence the way these activities develop.

Plane, car, train or boat?

European forecasts suggest that it will be up to the road system to absorb a large part of the 40% increase in the volume of passenger transport forseen between now and 2010. Air travel is also growing explosively for both business and tourism (forecast increase of 182% until 2010). Meanwhile, ecologically sound transport infrastructures such as cycle routes and waterways, both of which are strongly supported by the EU, will continue to be boycotted by potential users unless there is a major effort to convince the public of their value.

Source : Benelux Press.

Europe in action
Sustainable mobility

Europe will always have a growing demand for transport but is seeking to strike a more reasonable balance. It will, however, take time, money and a change in attitude (of which there is little sign as yet) if we are to get people out of their cars and onto trains or bikes.

Europe responded to steady traffic growth back in the early 1970s by declaring its intention to make vehicles cleaner and more fuel-efficient. The main instrument at the EU's disposal has been the introduction of new standards. Petrol and diesel cars, HGVs and oil tankers have all been subject to EU environmental regulations designed to reduce noise and emissions and to improve safety. For instance, new standards were agreed with manufacturers, which have helped reduce CO_2 emissions from road vehicles by making them more fuel-efficient. The clear success that has been achieved has encouraged both industry and EU to continue their efforts to further tailor these tools to the current situation (what can technology achieve and at what price?) and to the latest environmental objectives (what needs to be done to meet air quality standards, in order to protect public health - Auto-Oil programme).

More recently, the Commission has actively participated on the infrastructure front in the development of Trans-European transport Networks 'TEN'. Major projects of this kind, for which individual Member States are responsible, are designed to establish a better balance on the supply side (classic railway lines and high-speed links, roads, waterways, ports, airports, etc.) and to lighten the burden transport places on the environment. EU support of rail and combined (and public) transport is fully in line with its goal of sustainable mobility.

Inciting debate

The EU's aim of making users bear the full cost (including the ecological impact) of their transport decisions is encountering a great deal of resistance, as is the principle of green taxation. Everyone agrees that something ought to be done, but real action is invariably postponed. The EU is realistic about the problems that exist and has described the progress made so far as very weak.

Looking for new solutions

The EU has also strengthened its research and development policy by supporting a variety of different Community programmes, including one devoted to transport. Pilot studies into teleworking, the manufacture of electric cars and the enhanced organisation of urban transport have all been positively received at national and regional level.

Amsterdam Leidseplein. Source : Benelux Press.

The EU intends to continue along this path in the Framework Programme of Research and Development and has proposed research on transport systems that are economic, safe and protective of the environment and quality of life. This builds on initiatives to sketch the outlines of a 'new generation of aircraft', a 'train of the future' and a 'car of tomorrow'.

Setting the standard

Vehicles and fuels are subject to a variety of standards, the main aim of which is to reduce toxic emissions (exhaust gases) and to improve safety (regular technical inspection, advance notification of the transport of hazardous substances, etc.). Others relate to infrastructure (impact studies, compulsory distribution of unleaded petrol).

Infrastructure

The TEN embodies a fundamental objective of European transport policy, the execution of which would require an immense investment. In addition, EU subsidies to the transport sector could rise to ECU 25,000 million between 1994 and 1999 and credits to ECU 17,000 million.

Economic approach

The Commission has proposed measures that will take greater account of the true external costs of transport by obliging heavy goods vehicles, for instance, to meet the infrastructure and environment costs to which they give rise. Another item on the agenda is how to use vehicle tax to guide consumers towards cleaner and more fuel-efficient cars.

Brussels, Public transport.
Source : Benelux Press.

Developments

The Good... ...the Bad

- Technological progress.
- Development of the TEN.
- Increased awareness on the part of Member States and the public.
- Growth in transport.
- Privileged position enjoyed by roads.
- Economic incentives determined by considerations other than the environment.

Raising awareness

Everyone agrees that the current situation cannot continue. This view is reflected in the Green Paper on the impact of transport on the environment, and is reiterated in the White Paper on the future of common transport policy and the Transport Policy Action Plan 1995-2000, which sets out a timetable for the proposed actions. It is often difficult, however, to move from the initial recognition of the problem to concrete action. The problems are too intractable, the vested interests too numerous and the changes necessary too far-reaching.

Taking responsibility

Could Europe do more?

Further technological advances and the introduction of even more rigorous standards are not enough in themselves to counter the forecast increase in traffic and the implications of this for the environment. The EU will have to launch new initiatives to favour forms of transport that take better care of the environment. It also needs to ensure greater safety when hazardous goods are transported, to improve traffic management in the most sensitive areas and to use taxes in a way that encourages users and operators to make more reasonable choices. At infrastructure level, Europe should ensure that its financial support of schemes to adjust the transport mix are subjected to more critical evaluation. It could, in this regard, define a framework for the environmental viability of freight transport (combined road-rail).

Industrial responsibility

Much of what still remains to be done depends on the car and oil industries and on transport experts (improved vehicles, maintenance, 'green' logistics, etc.). The clearest example of this type of co-operation between the EU and industry is the 'Auto-Oil' programme, which is studying the most efficient measures for meeting the air quality standards fixed by the World Health Organisation. The introduction of the catalytic converter is the key achievement to date. Car manufacturers have also invested a great deal of time and money in R&D with a strong green feel - more fuel-efficient cars, recyclable materials and bodies that can be dismantled more easily at the end of the vehicle's useful life. The latest achievement is the use of interactive systems, such as computer programs that display the quickest alternative route in the event of traffic jams. All of this will benefit the environment and consumers.

On the right road

Many states have introduced measures to promote public transport. Several countries have taken a radical new line on infrastructure investment. The UK, for instance, has decided that expenditure on public transport should take precedence over that on roads. Member States have also launched information campaigns in an attempt to make public transport more attractive.

Convincing the user

Many of the policies introduced by Member States and the EU can only succeed if transport users modify their behaviour. Motorists bear a particular responsibility in this regard as they produce half of all the CO_2 emissions attributed to transport. We have to persuade motorists to use their cars more selectively and to choose vehicles that are less harmful to the environment. Transport users need precise consumer information on the ecological performance of vehicles if they are to be able to make more informed choices.

Local input

The principles of subsidiarity and shared responsibility are particularly relevant in the field of transport. A coherent approach requires that everybody - government, industry, transport companies and users - shares in the effort. Local decision-makers play a key role in shaping transport policies that show greater respect for the environment. They are stepping up their efforts to tackle the problem of congestion and pollution in urban centres. Tax incentives, efficient and accessible public transport, free provision of cycles and strategically placed car parks to allow effective links with public transport are just some of the steps that can help achieve this objective.

Conjestion on N25, UK.
Source : Michael St Maur Sheil.

Facts and Trends
A serious case of bulimia

Energy may be vital to our economic development, but it is also a gigantic source of environmental pollution. How can we reduce demand for energy at a time when oil prices are so low and our desire for comfort so high?

Almost every aspect of our daily lives depends on energy. Energy keeps us warm, fuels our cars and keeps our factories running. Problems in the energy supply or fluctuations in the price of fuel can have immense repercussions for the economy. This was made painfully clear by the spectacular price increases that occurred in the 1970s, pushing the West into recession.

Energy consumption, be it large or small in scale, is linked just as closely to fluctuations in the earth's ecological balance. Energy production is almost universally harmful to the environment, from extraction, transport and refining through to consumption. The risks can, however, be limited to some extent by the type of energy we choose (hydropower is a case in point).

Europe's economy has grown immensely since the early 1950s. We enjoy a standard of living previously undreamed of. This manifests itself in both industry and everyday life in the form of unbridled consumption - an inexorable rise in the number of cars, computers, washing machines and kilometres travelled. Europe's total gross inland consumption (not including the USSR) grew 74% between 1971 and 1990, from 770 to 1340 Mtoe. Although our machines have become more energy-efficient, higher consumption has combined with an increase in the number of households to produce a gradual but steady rise in demand for energy - roughly 0.6% a year between 1974 and 1992.

CO_2 in the dock

To put it bluntly, the rate at which demand for energy is growing is incompatible with the long-term survival of our planet. The hole in the ozone layer and acid rain are merely the most spectacular consequences of our voracious consumption of energy. CO_2 is the biggest villain. Massive quantities of the gas are pumped into the atmosphere by factory chimneys and car exhausts, making it one of the European Union's most pressing concerns. None of the measures taken so far has genuinely tackled the root of the problem. The price of oil has slipped back to an affordable level, sapping the will of domestic and industrial consumers to reduce their energy requirements. Nor have they shown much interest in alternative or renewable energies.

Spectacular jump

Demand for electricity grew by 2.7% a year in the period 1974-92. In response, the generators increased capacity by 42% between 1980 and 1992. The increase was spread across the different energy sources, but most of the slack was taken up by nuclear power, which now supplies 35% of all our electricity, almost matching the share accounted for by solid fuels. Hydropower, which is known for its non-polluting character, makes up barely 9% of total production. As for the risks associated with atomic energy, nuclear power stations have little impact on the environment when operating normally, but the issue of nuclear waste and its storage remains a key concern in today's Europe.

Yorkshire, UK.
Source: Benelux Press.

Europe in action

Greater cohesion

Europe decided at a very early stage to devote a considerable amount of money to improving the way it manages its energy consumption. The problem then arose of how to persuade the governments, manufacturers, producers, distributors and consumers in its Member States that they ought to coordinate their efforts more effectively.

Europe was equally quick to incorporate environmental concerns in its energy policy after the First Oil Crisis. Its motivation was simple: greater energy efficiency would simultaneously reduce environmental pollution and Europe's dependence on the oil-producing countries.

Although early measures to combat air pollution and acid rain failed to reduce total energy consumption in the EU, they at least managed to slow down the rate at which demand (gross inland consumption per unit of GDP) was increasing.

In more recent years, the EU has launched a series of common energy programmes to help meet the challenge of bringing CO_2 emissions back to their 1990 level by the year 2000. But these measures alone were still clearly not enough. The EU's next move was to create a set of new economic and fiscal weapons, which were brought to bear first of all on climate change. The most ambitious of the new instruments would be CO_2 energy tax. What's more, a great deal of the increase in energy consumption is attributable to countries outside the EU. To address this problem, large-scale economic stimulation packages have been targeted at the nations of Central and Eastern Europe and the newly independent states of the former USSR.

Partnership with energy suppliers

The EU has also introduced economic incentives to help transform gas and electricity distributors into service providers with a vested interest in improving energy efficiency. In a similar kind of partnership, the Commission has brokered a voluntary agreement between domestic appliance manufacturers.

What about renewable energies?

The pattern of energy production has changed over the past ten years. The share accounted for by solid fuels has declined, while that of natural gas and nuclear power has increased. The target for 2010 is merely to exceed a market share of 7.5% for renewable energies, compared to 5% in 1995. Despite vigorous promotion in the shape of a series of common energy programmes, renewable energies are developing slowly because of the higher costs, operating constraints (renewable solutions are extremely localised or require a great deal of space) and difficulties in getting beyond the trial stage. 95% of this type of energy comes from biomass and hydropower. Other solutions promoted by

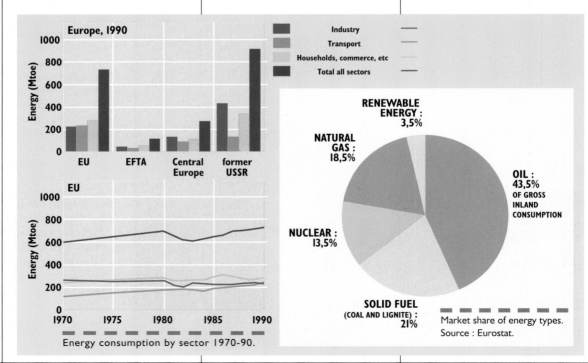

Energy consumption by sector 1970-90.

Market share of energy types.
Source : Eurostat.

Member States include bio-combustibles (in France and Finland), solar energy (Italy and the Netherlands), forestry waste (Denmark) and wind-farms (Greece and the Netherlands).

EU programmes

The JOULE THERMIE programme, launched in 1990, promoted new, non-polluting and efficient techniques for rational energy use, renewable energies, solid fuels and hydrocarbons. It was transformed in 1995 into a new programme for non-nuclear energy, designed to help reduce the adverse environmental impact of excessive energy consumption and to ensure sustainable energy sources at an affordable price.

SAVE 1 was launched in 1991 with the related goal of reducing CO_2 emissions. The aim of SAVE is also to improve energy management by actions at local and regional level and to develop new instruments capable of promoting improved energy efficiency.

ALTENER set out in 1993 to achieve the same goals via a different route - promoting renewable energies.

Developments
The Good...   ...the Bad

- Despite a series of EU programmes, CO_2 production in several sectors remains worrying.
- The use of renewable energies in most Member States has yet to advance beyond the research stage.
- Incentives to improve energy efficiency not only depend on specific government policies but also on the supply situation. France has a good record on CO_2 reduction, for instance, but this is chiefly due to the fact that it generates a large proportion of its electricity using nuclear power stations.
- Demand-side measures remain modest, despite national programmes to improve energy efficiency.
- The low energy prices we are currently witnessing may be good for economic development but are a powerful disincentive when it comes to saving energy.

It was only in 1995 that competitiveness and security of supply were added to the environmental aspect as key strands of the EU's common energy policy. The priority is now to ensure that the costs of energy production and consumption are integrated more effectively into market prices.

- - - - - - - - - -

Rapp-Bode dam, Saxony - Anhalt, Germany. Source : H. Lange, Bruce Coleman Ltd.

Taking responsibility

Long-term vision

Policies in this field have to be long-term in character if energy production and consumption are to be made less harmful to the environment. Europe intends to build on the achievements of existing policy while focusing on crucial factors like the forecast increase in traffic. New approaches were defined and presented in 1994 in a document entitled 'For a European Union Energy Policy'. The priorities set out at that time were to further develop clean technologies, to improve energy efficiency and to move towards a pricing system that takes full account of all the market's external costs.

Member States at work

EU governments are supporting the development of more efficient energy use. Germany, Denmark, Luxembourg, the Netherlands and Greece, for instance, are promoting techniques for combined heat and power production. On the demand side, national energy programmes have set targets for reducing energy consumption, but the measures actually taken remain very modest (insulating buildings, modernising public lighting, etc.). If the balance is to be corrected, these measures need to be linked with clear economic incentives. Specific agreements with large consumers are the most effective way of raising industry's awareness of the environmental issue. This is the approach France has adopted towards the steel, paper and paper pulp industries.

Mobilising Europe's citizens (again)

The oil crisis in the 1970s made Europe's citizens acutely aware of the need to conserve energy. This awareness has, however, weakened considerably in recent years as the price of oil returned to a more affordable level. Constant discipline is needed if we are to reduce the amount of fuel used by our central heating systems and cars. To address this problem, the EU has created local and regional energy management agencies. These are now active in quite a few Member States, where they support the efforts of gas and electricity distributors and local authorities to help members of the public make the right energy choices. The number of publications and members of staff devoted to this field is increasing. There is an interesting Spanish energy guide, for instance, which offers practical advice on the most effective use of household appliances, domestic heating and alternative energy. Meanwhile, Danish electricity bills include a detailed breakdown of power consumption which helps make customers more responsible.

Electricity pylons. Source : Atomic Energy Authority Culhan / Brooks, Krikler Research.

Facts and Trends

Agriculture and the environment - a marriage of convenience

Farmland and forests account for 42% and 33% respectively of all Europe's territory. There could hardly be a clearer indication of how our environment has been shaped by these landscapes. Farmers have traditionally been viewed as the gardeners and custodians of the countryside. Nevertheless, all manner of problems have frequently been laid at the farmer's door. The relationship between agriculture and the environment is complex, but we should never lose sight of the fact that farming itself also suffers from ecological damage - albeit sometimes self-inflicted.

Agriculture and forestry: environmental victims...

Atmospheric pollution, ozone build-up and climate change all affect growers' yields. Soil can suffer from erosion, compacting and reduced fertility, all of which are the result of excessive mechanisation on the farm, which can do irreparable damage to the very process it is meant to assist. In the space of 16 years, for instance, soil in the arable region of Beauce in France has lost half its organic matter. Our forests, too, are being damaged by pollution. One tree in four has been affected by acidification and tens of thousands of hectares are ravaged by fire every year.

... environmental threats

For many years, the main objectives of agricultural policy were self-sufficiency in food and steady growth in productivity. Nations needed to produce more and more all the time, causing them to invest successfully in mechanisation and research. Chemical fertilisers and pesticides did wonders for farmers' yields.

The countryside has been transformed to the detriment of existing ecosystems (hedgerows and copses). Characteristic habitats and general biodiversity have been lost and there have been other unwelcome consequences like soil erosion. Intensive use of fertilisers has adversely affected groundwater and encouraged eutrophication in surface waters. Intensive animal husbandry produces methane and ammonia and pollutes the atmosphere, while the immense quantities of liquid manure produced by agricultural firms have become an acute problem. Intensive irrigation and drainage practises also contribute to prominent problems such as water scarcity and loss of wetlands which have an important regulatory function in hydrologic concerns. Things aren't much better in our forests, where monoculture has again altered the landscape and reduced biodiversity. Human beings have long since exterminated all the large predators in our forests (wolf, lynx and bear).

Changing the face of agriculture

In the last few years, however, the trend has gradually reversed itself as governments and citizens alike have grown increasingly aware of the prevailing problems. The issue is no longer how to keep on producing more, but how to inflict less damage on the environment. For their part, consumers are demanding healthier and better quality products. Governments, meanwhile, have been encouraging forms of agriculture that are more beneficial to the environment, such as less intensive farming methods, organic cultivation and the maintenance and planting of hedgerows. Europe's total forested area has grown by 10% in the space of a few years.

Crop spraying in Germany.
Source : Michael St Maur Sheil.

# AGRICULTURE AND FORESTRY

Europe in action
A better understanding of the CAP

The Common Agricultural Policy (CAP) has long shaped the face of European farming. Before the 1992 reforms, the CAP was essentially based on a system of guaranteed prices (irrespective of demand), subsidies, investment incentives, import tariffs and research subsidies.

This approach encouraged excess production of cereals, beef, wine and dairy products. Quotas were introduced in the 1980s but these were still intended to guarantee prices rather than achieve any particular ecological advances.

It was only in 1985 that the European Community acknowledged the damage that agriculture can wreak on the environment. Since 1987, the CAP has adopted measures enabling, in particular, Member States to compensate farmers who set aside land from cultivation in sensitive zones.

The cost of the surpluses, that of storing and distributing them on the external markets and the macroeconomic imbalances

to which this gave rise, led to a major overhaul of the CAP in 1992. The aim was to reduce the surpluses and to go some way towards separating farmers' income from their output. Accordingly, the Commission proposes, in the future, to rely less and less on price support mechanisms, for they cannot guarantee farm incomes in the long-term.

Reconciling agriculture and the environment

Today's Common Agricultural Policy has to reconcile the needs of producers with environmental protection and maintenance of the rural standard of living. As regards the specific measures, they offer compensation or subsidies for:

- The use of less intensive methods: reducing pesticide and fertiliser inputs, for instance, and lowering the number of cattle per hectare;
- The transformation of arable land and pasture into

meadows;
- The development of methods to safeguard the quality of biotopes (planting and maintenance of hedgerows, maintenance of woods or copses);
- The long-term set-aside of farmland;
- Reforestation projects;
- Switching to organic farming.

Organic farming

Interest in non-intensive organic farming is growing as people begin to recognise the damage that intensive agriculture can cause to the environment and to people's health and as consumer demand for alternative, healthier products increases. However, organic agriculture is less productive which means that produce is often more expensive.

To avoid possible abuses, the European Community established a framework for the production and labelling of organic products.

Andalousia, Spain.
Source : Benelux Press.

38

Ploughed field. Adinkerke, Belgium.
Source : J. Herbauts.

Related policies

The objectives of the CAP are backed up by other directives, including those designed to protect our surface and groundwater - known collectively as the 'nitrates directive'. First adopted in 1991, this sets out to reduce the water pollution caused by nitrates used in farming and to prevent any new pollution of this type. To achieve this objective, the directive asks Member States to identify the surface area of their respective territories susceptible to pollution of this kind. Action programmes will then be established in those zones to reduce nitrogenous pollution at source. This will also entail Member States drafting codes of agricultural good practice.

A new framework directive on ground and surface water has been proposed which ought to provide solid protection for these waters throughout the European Union.

Forests

Huge areas of European forest are regularly burned down (1% a year). A EU regulation on fire-safety in forests allows at-risk zones to be identified and joint action plans to be approved.

The Fifth Programme projects an increase in the forested area and encourages a management approach that takes proper account of ecological needs.

Thousands of hectares of forest have suffered from acidification. The Community is addressing the direct causes of this problem by establishing standards for pollution generated by industry and the burning of fossil-fuels.

1992:
Reform of the CAP

The reforms recognised the environmental role played by agriculture and featured the following key elements:
- Reducing the role of the market and introducing progressively lower prices for agricultural produce;
- Establishing a guaranteed and direct income for farmers, independent of production levels, to compensate them for these reductions in price;
- Planning the compulsory set-aside of certain arable lands;
- Encouraging non-intensive husbandry of cattle and sheep;
- Maintaining certain quotas, such as those for milk and sugar;
- Supplementary measures including subsidies for tree planting and organic and non-intensive farming, and support for voluntary set-aside.

Taking responsibility

A code of good agricultural practice

In December 1991, the European Community adopted the directive on the protection of waters from nitrate pollution caused by farming (the 'nitrates directive'). Under the terms of the directive, Member States will draw up codes of good agricultural practice for nitrate fertilisation.

These codes will reflect reality on the ground as they attempt to ensure the proper use of chemical or organic fertilisers. The measures are voluntary for farmers, except where the activities in question take place in a zone designated as sensitive.

Member States will also continue the EU's pursuit of CAP reform by introducing agricultural and environmental measures tailored to the local situation and, in some cases, programmes of their own. Regional and municipal government can help promote the application of these measures by providing subsidies or by awarding farmers specific ecological labels.

Consumers

Citizens are consumers with an influence on demand, which means their behaviour can help shape the supply of agricultural produce and, by extension, farming practices themselves. They can choose free-range chickens rather than battery-raised ones, unprocessed fruit rather than graded, and seasonal vegetables rather than ones 'forced' with doses of fertiliser. They can also opt for organic products. Although these choices are not always easy on the wallet, they are beneficial to health and can have a modest impact on farming practices.

Through the choices they make, consumers can encourage agricultural producers to take better care of the environment.
Source : Eurostat.

Forests

Forests are renewable resources, but only in the very long term. European Member States have taken care for some time now to ensure that their woodland resources are managed sustainably by introducing rules that require replanting after felling. Such care is particularly important in mountainous areas, which are vulnerable to avalanches and erosion. Subsidies are available to encourage landowners to replant certain categories of farmland with trees, but these have not been very successful (not least because it takes a hundred years to reap the harvest).

International co-operation in the forestry field dates back some way. This is particularly the case with research, which has been headed since 1980 by the International Association of Forestry Research Organisations. More recently, the second Ministerial Conference on the Protection of Forests was held in Helsinki in June 1993, when 45 countries, inspired by the Rio Summit, undertook to do all in their power to promote the sustainable development of Europe's forests and to conserve their biodiversity.

Oilseed rape.
Source : Michael St Maur Sheil.

Facts and Trends
Fisheries : an essential economy

Marine fishing is an important economic activity in the European Union even though it employs only a limited number of people. The EU's 260,000 fishermen and women account for much less than 1% of its working population, but their activities are supported by a number of other commercial and manufacturing sectors such as boatbuilding and the processing and distribution of fish and fish products.

Denmark, Spain and the United Kingdom are the major marine fishing nations of the European Union.

Commercial fishing in freshwater is of limited importance within the European Union although it is of local importance in Sweden and Finland.

Recent increase in fishing

Fishing, both in European Union waters and elsewhere, became more intensive from the 1960's as European and world demand for fish increased and as markets diversified and became more readily available. The intensification was also promoted by the availability of relatively cheap fuel for fishing vessels, together with the use of more sophisticated technology, both in the design of nets and of navigational and fish-finding devices.

As a result, many of the fish stocks exploited by the vessels of the European Union are too heavily fished. Sometimes, they may even not be able to replenish themselves.

Fewer large, old fish are now available. Many fisheries therefore direct their activities towards the smaller, younger fish.

There is also the search for previously unexploited resources on species which inhabit deep waters over the continental slope and/or the abyssal plains which has led to the development of fisheries. These species have low reproductive and growth rates and may therefore rapidly become severely depleted.

It's not only about fish...

One associated effect of fishing includes changes in the species composition of the biological communities and changes of the size and age composition within many affected species.

Species other than those for which the fisheries have an economic interest or major dependency are also caught. These include marine mammals (mainly small whales, dolphins, porpoises and seals), marine birds and marine reptiles (mainly turtles). Also caught are some fish species, such as sturgeon, whose populations are considered to be in an endangered state. Some types of fishing may disrupt communities of invertebrate animals which live in or on the seabed.

The severe depletion of populations of monk seal is partly due to accidental or deliberate killing by fishermen and by reduction in availability of appropriate food as a result of increased fishing activity. However, loss of suitable breeding habitat as a result of the development of coastal tourism has also contributed to the problem.

Aquaculture

Fish and fish products are also increasingly produced by aquaculture in the hope to help offset the overall decline in production from the wild fish stocks exploited by conventional fisheries.

However, the practice of aquaculture is not free from potentially adverse environmental effects. These sometimes manifest themselves as eutrophication or deoxygenation of areas in the vicinity of aquaculture establishments which may be caused by the release of effluents from such plants.
In addition, escapes of exotic species or specifically bred stocks of indigenous species may cause a problem.

Fisheries ... also a victim

There may also be negative effects of pollution on fish or aquaculture, either by direct mortality of fish or by various debilitating processes such as reduction in reproductive potential. Conversely, it has been claimed that influx of phosphates has, in some geographical areas such as the North Sea, fertilised these areas and has resulted, inter alia, in increased production of at least some fish species.

Europe in action
Towards solutions

A Common Fisheries Policy

The future of fishing fundamentally depends on the future of the fish themselves. Recognition of this fact prompted the European Community to develop a policy of sustainable development with respect to the exploitation of fish stocks which is intended to reconcile

Artic charr. Source : P. S. Maitland

the legitimacy of exploiting fish stocks with the need to conserve such stocks.

Zones and quotas

In 1977, most of the world's nations, including the current EU Member States, established Exclusive Economic Zones.

These zones gave to these nations exclusive rights on a number of issues, including fishing, within 200 nautical miles from their respective coastlines.

In 1983, a number of Total Allowable Catches (TAC's) for the major fish stocks in the waters of the Community was established. The Council also agreed upon allocation of these TAC's among Member States as national quotas under a system which became known as relative stability.

The relative stability system allocates fixed and agreed percentages of TAC's to Member States.
In principle, TAC's and quotas control the output from fisheries and this should be sufficient to ensure sustainability.

However, the existence of «mixed fisheries » in which many fishes are caught simultaneously, gives rise to problems with respect to overshooting TAC's.

Fishing for ship sturgeon, Volga.
Source : W. Fisher, WWF.

Fishing in the North Sea.
Source : Frank Spooner Pictures.

Control of fishing effort

In 1992, against the background of increasing rates of exploitation and hence of increasing risk to the sustainability of fish stocks, other tools were developed among which the direct control of fishing effort.

To control fishing effort, therefore, we have introduced control of "kilowatt-days" or some equivalent quantity.

Control of the capacity of the fleets

In addition to direct control of fishing effort, Member States have recognised that many of their fishing fleets are simply too large.

In response to this problem, Member States have participated in a series of Multi-Annual Guidance Programmes (MAGP) by which the size of all or some of their fleets will be reduced by agreed amounts.

Parallel social and economic measures have been introduced to alleviate the transition to smaller fleets and reduced fishing effort.

East-Friesian Wadden Sea, Germany.
Source : D. Wascher.

Taking responsibility

Technical measures

Since 1984, a package of technical measures has been in place for fisheries in the north-east Atlantic. These measures define, inter alia, minimum mesh sizes of nets and closed areas and closed seasons primarily intended for the protection of juvenile fish.

For the Baltic, a similar package has been in existence since 1986.

The Mediterranean

In the Mediterranean, no Exclusive Economic Zones have been established. Because of this and because of the highly multispecific nature of catches in many of the fisheries, especially by trawls or similar fishing methods, no TAC and quota system has been established.

However, in 1994, the Council adopted a regulation defining technical measures applicable to the vessels of Member States whether fishing within their own territorial limits or beyond. The Multi-Annual Guidance Programmes also apply to Community fleets fishing within the Mediterranean.

The European Union has also organised two International Diplomatic Conferences, in 1994 and 1996, on the management of Mediterranean fish stocks which were attended by all Mediterranean States.

Reduction of coincidental catches

It can be reasonably expected that reduction in fishing effort and the size of fleets should lead to reduction in coincidental catches of birds, mammals, reptiles, etc. even though this is not always specifically mentioned in the legal texts.

More thought needs still to be given to establishing conditions for the protection of those species taken by fishing gears but which are not required by fishermen. Also to be considered is the possibility of establishing conditions to minimise the risk of food deprivation for marine birds and mammals.

Control and enforcement

It would be naive to expect fishermen at sea to automatically obey Community Regulations and therefore a regulation has been put in place simply which is why a regulation dealing specifically with the monitoring and control of fishing activities has been put into place.

Each Member State monitors and controls the activities of vessels of their own or other Member States or of third country vessels. The European Commission also employs its own inspectors.

The skippers of any Community fishing vessel of length greater than 10 metres have to keep a log-book to record, in particular, the quantities of each species caught and the amount retained on board. Specific requirements are also in force with respect to declaration of landings at ports and recording sales at auction centres and elsewhere.

Large, highly mobile vessels (greater than 20 metres overall length) now have to carry satellite monitoring devices.

The future

The European Commission recognises 2002 as a suitable date by which to implement possible modifications and augmentations of the Common Fisheries Policy. and is already preparing the ground for a wide-ranging discussion with administrations of Member States and with all other interested parties.

It is difficult to predict in detail the precise outcome of this discussion. However, it should be recalled that, throughout the world, all management systems for the conservation of fish stocks include some combination of TAC's and quotas, effort control and technical measures.

Monitoring in the Mediterranean.
Source : Frank Spooner Pictures.

Facts and Trends

The hazards of the consumer society

Holding back domestic consumption is no easy matter, especially at a time when the number of households is expanding so quickly (not to mention their appetite for goods and services). The earth, which has to support them all, has come close to throwing in the towel.

European households (that is, groups of people sharing the same living space) monopolise 5-30% of water supplies, 15-20% of electricity consumption and over 70% of manufactured goods. Mass consumption on this scale has transformed households into key economic players, but also means that they have a significant impact on the environment. Pressure is exerted at two distinct stages - consumer demand places an intense burden on natural resources, while the manufacture, use and disposal of consumer goods pollute the water, air and soil. Some 75% of European households, for instance, have at least one car - a figure that has risen by 20% since 1985. These generate 5% of SO_2 emissions (both vehicular and otherwise) and 10% of volatile organic compounds (heating and cars).

Sadly, this situation is unlikely to improve in the years to come. It is true that more and more European citizens are realising that by consuming more selectively and wasting less, they can reduce the harm they do to the environment. Important as this new awareness is, though, it cannot outweigh the overall growth in the purchasing power of the average European citizen.

Consumers as a pressure group

When it comes to persuading manufacturers to adopt cleaner industrial processes and to reduce the environmental impact of their operations, consumers have a formidable weapon at their disposal in that they can refuse to place certain products in their supermarket trolleys. Households can thus exert a significant influence on the different sectors of the economy when making their everyday choices from amongst the well-filled shelves of the local superstore.

European statistics reveal that citizens' ecological awareness has risen in line with their household income. In other words, and at the risk of seeming to contradict what was said above about how higher income means increased consumption of goods and services, the richer we are, the more ecological we could become in our consumer behaviour. A range of other factors is also at play. Take the issue of 'size'. We know that smaller households (an established trend) use relatively more energy and water and occupy more land (per person) as they do not achieve the economies of scale of larger households.

--- --- --- --- --- --- --- ---

What actions have European citizens taken or would they consider taking to safeguard the environment ? 70% of respondents said that they had already bought ecological products or would do so, even if they were more expensive. (EU, 1992). Source: CEC, 1992 b.

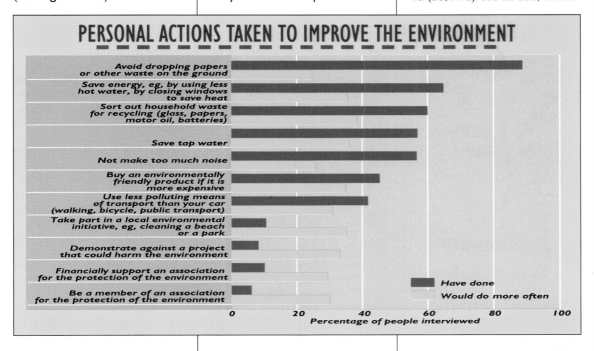

PERSONAL ACTIONS TAKEN TO IMPROVE THE ENVIRONMENT

- Avoid dropping papers or other waste on the ground
- Save energy, eg, by using less hot water, by closing windows to save heat
- Sort out household waste for recycling (glass, papers, motor oil, batteries)
- Save tap water
- Not make too much noise
- Buy an environmentally friendly product if it is more expensive
- Use less polluting means of transport than your car (walking, bicycle, public transport)
- Take part in a local environmental initiative, eg, cleaning a beach or a park
- Demonstrate against a project that could harm the environment
- Financially support an association for the protection of the environment
- Be a member of an association for the protection of the environment

■ Have done
□ Would do more often

Percentage of people interviewed

Europe in action
Key players

Europe decided that if it was to reduce the harmful impact of domestic consumption on the environment, it had to regulate production more effectively. Early results were not satisfactory, however, and so a change of tack was needed. The EU's current approach is to try and involve all the relevant players in its strategy.

Households have always been key players in environmental policy because of the holidays they take, the gas they consume to keep themselves warm, the cars they buy to get them around and their love affair with shopping. This fact has not always been taken fully into account, however, by the powers-that-be. Although they have been targeted indirectly by measures to control vehicle emissions and fuel consumption, to improve energy efficiency and to reduce waste-generation, private citizens have never been placed at the centre of European programmes in this field. Policies have tended to be aimed instead at the producers of goods and services. The period 1990-

95 was very significant in this regard as it saw the development of technologies and products capable of reducing the burden placed on the environment (catalytic converters, unbranded products, CFC-free products, etc).

Direct approach to raise awareness

A series of measures has been introduced, for example, to promote the benefits of more environmentally friendly products such as washing machines that consume less water, central-heating boilers that use less fuel and quieter dishwashers. Similarly, a European Eco-label has been introduced for washing machines, dishwashers, fertilisers, toilet paper, kitchen roll, washing powders and liquids, light-bulbs, paints and varnish, bed-linen and T-shirts, writing paper, fridges and freezers. There is a European energy label, too, and national Eco-labels. Consumers can also choose from a wide range of products labelled or certified as 'ecological' according to less regulated criteria.

Brief review of actions

1. CONTROLS
   These have proved their effectiveness in a range of everyday fields, from home insulation, improved water management

and the creation of no-smoking areas to the reduction of CFC compounds in the manufacture of consumer goods and municipal collection and sorting of recyclable goods.

2. EUROPEAN ECO-LABEL
   Even though very few products have yet been awarded a European Eco-label, consumers ought to be aware of its existence. It takes the form of a star-studded daisy and is the only label of its kind in the 15 countries of the Union to test ecological quality so rigorously. Labels are awarded to products that meet certain criteria defined by an environmental study, that have been accredited by a national certification body and that undergo a three-yearly review to ensure that all the criteria are still being met.

3. ECO-TAXES
   The EU supports the ambitious idea of taxing polluting products to encourage consumers and manufacturers to switch to less harmful alternatives. Experience in a number of cases has been extremely positive, with behaviour successfully modified in the desired way. An example is lead-free petrol, which made its first appearance in 1986 and now accounts for over 60% of the market There has been a continuing increase in the use of environmental taxes over the last decade, which has accelerated in the last 5 years. It also appears that most of the taxes have achieved their environmental objectives at reasonable cost.

Community eco-label award scheme

4. INFORMATION

Information has become increasingly transparent and accessible at local, regional and national level thanks to the directive on freedom of access to environmental data. The Directive represents a dramatic change for most Member States, introducing openness where secrecy was the rule. Four years of experience have shown, however, that the process of change is a gradual one and that continued progress, both in terms of the quantity and the quality of the information available, is still desirable.

Source : Benelux Press

Developments

The Good...   ...the Bad

- A more aware and better informed public is becoming more demanding;
- Improved energy-efficiency in the domestic field;
- Scientific and technical advances;
- All the indicators show that consumption of raw materials, energy, transport and tourist services is continuing to grow remorselessly;
- Demographic growth and shrinkage in the size of households.

Taking responsibility

Europe changes its target

Europe understands that it is consumers and no longer just manufacturers who hold the key to the problem of the environment. For that reason, EU policies to reduce ecological damage in the run-up to the year 2000 have shifted their focus to private citizens. The goal is to reduce domestic consumption of energy, water and transport by encouraging households to adopt habits that are more in line with the principle of sustainable development. This will be a particularly difficult challenge to meet, not least because of the significant number of parties involved. Europe also has to communicate with its citizens in a way that is acceptable to everyone. While it must be honest about the problems, it cannot afford to be alarmist. It also has to overcome the reluctance generated by the prospect of higher prices. The use of eco-taxes, for instance, is far from generally accepted as yet.

Responsible manufacturers

Industry has made substantial ecological advances in recent years under pressure from politicians and consumers. It must now continue along the path of clean production by agreeing a series of environmental accords with national governments, undertaking to respect the codes of conduct drawn up by its various federations.

Enhanced information and education

Although Europe has improved access to environmental information, it is up to national and local governments to put the principle of transparency truly into practice. Sweden has achieved a great deal in this area. The government has ensured that full details are now available regarding hazardous substances, but has also allowed citizens to mount their own actions, boycotting certain products, demanding better labelling, but also engaging in dialogue with the chemical industry. Consumer organisations like 'Which' in the UK and 'Que choisir?' in France can also make a positive social contribution in this respect, alongside their direct campaigning.

Consuming more responsibly

If there is a demand, producers are sure to meet it. Consumers like ourselves have grown accustomed to certain comforts from which we will find it difficult to wean ourselves. Paper handkerchiefs and individual portions of cake are just so handy. Other than convenience, however, there is very little to justify our current obsession with throw-away products and individual servings.

Source : Benelux Press.

Facts and Trends
Greening the tourist

Tourism's mission is to become the European Union's premier economic activity by the end of the century. It is vital, however, that the sector manages its development more responsibly. Greater respect for the environment is the first item on the list.

Tourism has grown exponentially over the past thirty years. The reasons aren't difficult to find: substantially improved road networks, more disposable cash for holidays and ever-cheaper air travel. Not to mention the opening up of international frontiers and a plethora of travel information. Europe is an extremely popular holiday destination for foreign tourists. The number of arrivals rose from 200 to 300 million between 1980 and 1990. Tourism currently generates no less than 5.5% of the European Union's total GNP. It is a fully-fledged industry that delivers jobs and economic development. When it is poorly managed, however, or allowed to get out of hand, tourism becomes another major source of pollution. The negative effects are varied and complex. Tourism can damage air and water quality, put pressure on traditional habitats, promote deforestation and generate large volumes of waste. At the same time, its future development is intimately bound up with the quality of the environment. The tourism industry has a direct interest in pursuing a strategy compatible with the objectives of sustainable development. No tourist wants to swim in water that smells bad or to visit a dead forest.

An economic issue

The future development of Europe's tourist industry depends on political stability, a sound economy and steadily increasing leisure time. The sector is forecast to grow by almost 6% annually until the year 2000. Other important trends include:
- steady growth in all regions;
- Central and Eastern Europe and the Eastern Mediterranean will experience vigorous growth in tourism;
- an increasing number of tourists from Southern Europe are visiting the North;
- the number of people visiting tourist sites hit by environmental problems (the Alps and the Mediterranean, for instance) is declining;
- the number of car and plane journeys is increasing;
- interest in green tourism and short-haul holidays is growing;
- a wide range of tourist opportunities and services are on offer;
- costs are falling.

Tourism in the Alpes
Source : Benelux Press

From seashore to mountain top

It goes without saying that pollution does not affect all tourist locations in the same way. Natural parks, mountains, coastal resorts, rural areas, towns and theme parks offer hundreds of different activities. You can only ski in the mountains and the impact of this activity (soil erosion, deforestation, infrastructure building) is totally different to the damage wrought by those who prefer seaside holidays (destruction of dunes, deteriorating water quality, etc.). Within these categories, however, there are a number of constants when it comes to the underlying causes of pollution: large numbers of visitors, seasonal concentrations, type of transport, real-estate pressures and so on. Cities are other blackspots. Not only are their own inhabitants responsible for a great deal of pollution, they are becoming increasingly popular tourist destinations. This poses the danger of additional air and noise pollution in urban areas and threatens our historic monuments.

Europe in action

A multi-disciplinary approach

The EU does not have any specific remit for the tourism sector, but can influence environmental management in areas as varied as water, transport, waste and infrastructure financing.

The Fifth Environmental Action Programme does not set any specific targets in terms of tourism. It does, however, consider the following to be necessary:
1/ A genuine dialogue with Member States regarding transport policy.

2/ Promotion of alternative forms of transport (greater use of public transport). Examples include tax measures to discourage citizens from using their cars, toll roads, traffic taxes and fuel taxes.

3/ Pollution control by reducing emissions, waste, etc.

Europe's Tourism Support Action Plan sponsors a number of sustainable tourism

pilot projects. They include integrated management plans for the North Sea coast and a programme to conserve Ireland's landscape heritage. The Commission has initiated a European Tourism and Environment Prize to encourage the industry to pay greater respect to the natural and cultural environment.

Additional measures

Other measures can also help directly or indirectly to reduce tourism's environmental impact. Environmental quality standards for drinking water, bathing water, wastewater and atmospheric emissions have been incorporated in European Directives. The Blue Flag campaing is linked to the respect of the strictest quality standards of the Bathing Water Directive. Only the best environmentally managed beaches - clealiness, environmental education, accomodation and water quality - are awarded the Blue Flag. The public have become more and more aware about this initiative as the years have gone by.
Europe has also had a major influence on the tourism industry by promoting more environmentally friendly infrastructure projects. The Structural Fund has devoted over three billion ecu to co-financing transport, water-treatment and waste-management projects in four countries (Spain, Portugal, Greece and Ireland). Part of the LIFE programme also involves projects relating to the protection and management of coastal zones and wastewater processing.

The 'Blue Flag' initiative is a perfect example of a non-gouvernemental project linking public health concerns, Europe's desire to manage tourist sites environmentally and the tourism sector's interest in protecting its natural assets over the long term. Source : Michael St Maur Sheil.

Beefing up environmental impact assessments

The EU has proposed several amendments to 1985's Environmental Impact Assessment Directive. These studies have now been extended to 'potentially harmful' tourist projects, such as ski runs, artificial snow machines, golf courses, holiday villages, hotel complexes, leisure centres and campsites.

Trial runs

Managing tourist infrastructure, raising public awareness and training operators were all tried out first at local, regional or national level. Limiting bed capacity or tourist numbers (certain national parks, islands and historic sites) and restrictions on new building are all examples of planning measures taken by the relevant authorities, which can call on both national regulations and the European Environmental Impact Assessment Directive.

Developments
The Good...   ...the Bad

- Public and industry awareness of the dangers of mass tourism.
- Development of eco-tourism.
- More responsible management of tourism at Member-State level (awarding of tourist 'eco-labels').
- Development of new, more environmentally friendly tourist activities.
- The exponential growth of the tourism sector.
- The undermining of environmental policies in sensitive areas by tourist activities.
- The tourism sector's environmental impact can't be fully evaluated because of the fragmentary nature of the available information.
- Lack of a clear regional strategy for promoting a more environmentally friendly tourism.

EU programmes and the European Social Fund have supported a series of ventures, including the guides to good practice published by hotel chains and auto-mobile clubs and the improved training of tourist staff.

Piazza San Marco, Venice.   Source : G. Arici, Grazia Neri, Milan.

Taking responsibility

Taking a long view

European finance (particularly the Cohesion Fund) will have an immense influence on the way tourism develops in the years to come thanks to its involvement in trans-European transport networks, water-treatment and waste-management infrastructures and habitat protection.

A common strategy

It is up to the regions to develop a clear strategy to nurture 'Green Tourism'. Their closest ally in this process will be the tourism industry itself, which will help the various regional bodies to encourage the diversification of tourist activities and to manage mass tourism more effectively. This will be done first and foremost by improving service quality and by encouraging a positive change in tourist behaviour. But information campaigns and codes of conduct alone are not enough if we are to persuade the public to pay more respect to an environment which, by definition, is not familiar to them. The only way to get tourists to leave their beloved cars behind is by offering them the opportunity to travel by train, bus or boat.

The battle goes on

The policy initiatives launched by Member States in recent years have generally been designed to take better account of the environmental impact of tourism. This has led, for instance, to improvements in the road infrastructure. Although initiatives of this kind allow us to restrict access to certain highly sensitive zones and to manage congestion more effectively during the great holiday exodus, they have had little impact on tourist numbers or the areas they overrun. If anything, they have had the contrary effect. For that reason, we will have to follow the French example and encourage tourism to alternative destinations or at alternative times of year.

The public's tastes are changing

The number of European and international tourists is growing all the time. Fortunately, many of them are also showing signs of more responsible behaviour. There is clear interest, for example, in new types of leisure (visits to natural parks, rural gîtes and holiday farms, eco-tourism) which integrate more harmoniously with the local economy. These account for a substantial proportion of the wider range of destinations now on offer and the gradual spreading out of holiday periods. These new converts to nature must understand, however, that an unbridled rush into the countryside could put Europe's wildest regions at risk (especially the Far North and Russia). The behaviour of such tourists is often contradictory. Although they display a growing ecological awareness, they have a taste for sporting activities that are eating up more and more of our unspoiled countryside in the name of thrills rather than that of communing with nature.

Amsterdam, NL. Source : Benelux Press.

CLIMATE CHANGE

OZONE LAYER

ACIDIFICATION

AIR QUALITY

Facts and Trends
Things are hotting up

The average temperature on the earth's surface remained relatively stable for 10,000 years. In the last hundred years, however, human activities have been generating steadily growing amounts of what we now know as 'greenhouse gases'. These have altered the composition of the atmosphere and have raised the average temperature on the surface of the earth. Though difficult to forecast with any precision, the potential consequences of this are alarming as they include phenomena such as changes in rainfall patterns and the level of the oceans.

The 'natural' greenhouse effect

The atmosphere that surrounds us creates a 'natural' greenhouse effect around the earth. The gases of which it is composed absorb the sun's rays and give off heat, just like the glass in a greenhouse. Without them, the average temperature on the earth's surface would be no higher than minus 18 degrees. All the water would be frozen solid and the planet would be uninhabitable.

Upset balance

Since the beginning of the century, a considerable increase in energy consumption in the industrialised countries has begun to reinforce this natural greenhouse effect in a potentially dangerous way. The main culprit is the CO_2 generated by the burning of fossil fuels (oil, coal and natural gas). The average concentration of CO_2 in the atmosphere is forecast to double in the course of the next century. If this were to occur, a temperature rise of around 2.5 degrees would be experienced over the next hundred years, compared to only half a degree during the last hundred.

Source : Dobris.

What are the effects?

The repercussions of global warming are still difficult to predict, but current evidence suggests that it might have an immense impact on sea level, the natural variability of the climate and rainfall patterns (more severe droughts and flooding), which would pose a grave threat to agriculture, forestry and ecosystem functionalities.

Reducing the harm

Scientists calculate that if the terrestrial ecosystem is to be able to adapt to these variations in climate, temperatures cannot rise by more than 0.1 degrees and the sea level by more than 2 cm in the space of any ten-year period. To stay within these limits, however, world emissions of greenhouse gases would have to be slashed by 60% overnight!

It is clearly impossible to achieve this objective, but that in no way reduces the need for us to act quickly. Not least because greenhouse gases remain in the atmosphere for a considerable time, which means they will continue to have an effect, even after they cease to be emitted.

GAS	ORIGIN	CONTRIBUTION TO GREENHOUSE EFFECT
CO_2 (carbon dioxide)	Energy consumption (80%), deforestation (17%)	51%
CH_4 (methane)	Energy production and consumption (26%), fermentation (24%), paddy-fields (17%)	34%
CFC & HCFC	Industry (100%)	12%
N_2O (nitrous oxide)	Fertilisers (48%), land clearance (17%)	4%

Europe in action
An immense challenge

The battle against climate change is one of the key ecological challenges facing European policy, which has established targets for significant reductions in greenhouse gas emissions. These are proving difficult to meet, however, particularly because of the growth of road traffic and the slow progress being made by some member states.

The energy sector contributes the most to global warming. As the producer of 80% of CO_2 emissions and 26% of methane emissions, it has inevitably been the primary target for the range of European regulations introduced in this field in recent years.

- 1992 - Europe signs up for Rio.
  The UN Earth Summit at Rio de Janeiro produced the first international agreement in the field of climate change. More than 150 countries signed up to a framework convention obliging them to take control of their greenhouse gas emissions. More specifically, Europe, together with other developed countries, undertook at Rio to stabilise emissions at their 1990 level by the year 2000.

- 1995, more conferences. Europe asserts itself.
  All the countries that signed up to the Convention come together at regular intervals to evaluate progress, redefine their commitments, set new objectives for the years beyond 2000 and adopt new policies to help them achieve these objectives. The first signatories' conference took place in Berlin in 1995 and the second in Geneva in 1996. On each occasion, Europe showed a determination to redouble its efforts, despite the rather unsatisfactory results achieved so far. In concrete terms, it has proposed the following actions:
- More generalised use of renewable energy.
- Changing patterns of trans-
port use.
- Increasing energy taxes.
- Improving the fuel-efficiency of cars.
- Promoting research into new technology.
- Strengthening co-operation with other countries.

- 1997, Kyoto.
  Third conference of signatories to the International Convention on climate change signed at Rio in 1992 by over 150 states. For its part, Europe decided in March 1997 to reduce its emissions of greenhouse gases by 15% of 1990 levels by 2010. The challenge it faces at Kyoto is to persuade other states outside the EU to adopt a similar commitment.

Energy taxes and carbon taxes: the best way forward

The purpose of taxing CO_2 emissions is to encourage the use of less polluting fuels and to promote more rational energy use. Analysts calculate that only by introducing such a tax will we be able to achieve the objectives to which Europe is committed. The tax would apply to varying degrees to oil, coal, natural gas and electricity, with scope for exempting certain industries (steel, chemicals, cement and paper).
This project has not received maximum support in the Member States. The debate goes on.

Five programmes to save energy

A variety of programmes have

Source : Benelux Press

been set up since the beginning of the 1990s to reduce Europe's energy consumption. Within this overall objective, they set out to develop and promote:

- Thermal insulation of buildings and the inspection of central-heating boilers.
- Use of renewable energy (wind, wave and biomass power).
- Special labels for freezers, refrigerators, washing machines and tumble-dryers that use less energy.

What results?

Various studies have attempted to calculate whether Europe's targets for the year 2000 will be met or not. Forecasts vary widely, but Europe appears to be making general progress towards its goals, even if it might not meet them in full. A number of factors have encouraged this trend, the most important being weaker than anticipated economic growth.

Developments

The Good... ...the Bad

- National programmes to reduce CO_2 emissions.
- Evaluation and restriction of these emissions by Member States.
- Improved energy-efficiency of certain appliances.
- Restrictions on use of fossil fuels.
- Development of renewable energy.
- Increasing road traffic.
- Energy prices do little to discourage consumption.
- Growing use of non-renewable energy sources;
- Delays in the application of national and European programmes.
- Lack of enthusiasm on the part of certain countries (developing nations, for instance).

After a period of steady growth, CO_2 emissions fell between 1990 and 1993, partly because of the recession. Since then, emissions have started to climb again. Whether or not we can succeed in stabilising emissions will depend on a number of positive and negative developments. Source : IPCC, 1990.

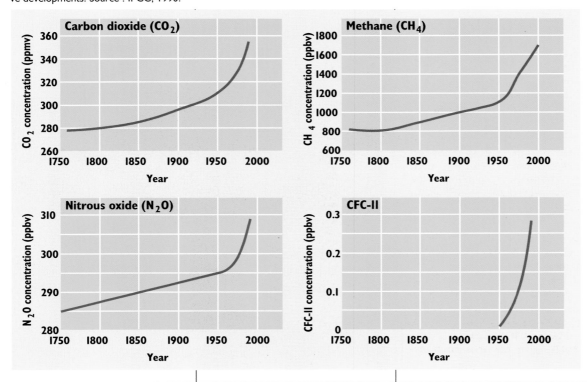

Taking responsibility

Balance needed at international level

Tackling climate change in an effective manner will require a high level of international co-operation. Three quarters of greenhouse gas emissions are currently generated by one quarter of the world's population (US, Europe and Japan). Steady economic development means, however, that countries like India and China could substantially increase their emissions of greenhouse gases. For that reason, we have to find a balance at global level that will share the necessary effort fairly between the countries, depending on each one's relative needs and their responsibility for the problem.

Some European countries more resolute than others

Following the ratification of the framework convention on climate change, each EU member state drafted its target for reducing greenhouse gas emissions, the methods to be adopted and an action plan. Some states adopted targets more ambitious than those fixed by Europe, but others asked for more time in which to meet even the EU goals. The progress achieved by the different countries is evaluated every year by the Commission.
What's more, the European Union has stated that it is prepared to reduce greenhouse gas emissions to 85% of their 1990 level by the year 2010.

Emissions from steelworks, Gijon, Spain. Source : Simon Fraser/Science Photo Library.

Don't change the climate, change attitudes

Citizens can help resist climate change. Household energy-savings have so far been marginal, but there are a number of ways in which people can contribute:
- By using electricity and heating more sensibly.
- Reducing individual transport.
- Choosing domestic appliances carefully (looking for the energy label).
- Improving thermal insulation;
- Choosing gas central-heating rather than oil.
- Using renewable energy.

Business remains reluctant

Energy-conservation programmes (THERMIE, SAVE, JOULE) and environmental management systems (EMAS) have encouraged some action in the industrial sector, but a great deal more progress is required than has been achieved to date. Industry will no doubt be more inclined to adopt energy-efficient technologies when doing so begins to have a beneficial impact on profits (i.e. when the price of energy starts to rise). Meanwhile, industry is fighting to keep energy costs as low as possible, citing the danger of lost competitiveness in world markets.

Current contributions of the different greenhouse gases to the enhanced greenhouse effect. Source : IPCC, 1990.

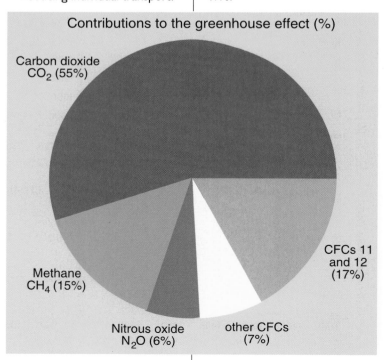

Contributions to the greenhouse effect (%)

Carbon dioxide CO_2 (55%)

CFCs 11 and 12 (17%)

Methane CH_4 (15%)

Nitrous oxide N_2O (6%)

other CFCs (7%)

Facts and Trends
Sunstroke on a global scale

The ozone layer is a vital protective shield located between 10 and 50 km above the earth's surface. Its most important function, as far as terrestrial life is concerned, is to filter out harmful UV rays contained in sunlight. The gradual formation of the ozone layer enabled life on earth to evolve in the first place, so it's not hard to imagine how disastrous it would be for both humanity and all the planet's ecosystems if our protective shield were to be seriously damaged.

Turning back the tide

It was back in 1970 that scientists first predicted that the ozone layer was thinning. Fifteen years later, an actual hole was detected above the Antarctic. The damage has been done by a range of human-manufactured chemicals, especially gases containing chlorine or bromine atoms. It can take these atoms ten years to find their way into the upper atmosphere, but once there, they spend many more years reacting with and destroying thousands of ozone molecules. It only takes small amounts of gas to produce this delayed effect. Even if CFC and halon emissions had stopped completely in 1995, the ozone layer would have continued to deteriorate until 2050. Every five-year delay in the total elimination of these substances adds another eighteen years to the ongoing destruction of the ozone layer, making rapid preventative measures more vital than ever.

UV, people and nature

As the ozone layer grows thinner, the amount of ultraviolet B (UV-B) radiation getting through to the earth's surface increases. UV-B creates a whole range of hazards. It affects the health of humans, animals, plants, micro-organisms, construction materials and air quality. Cataracts, skin cancer, genetic damage and a weakened immune system are just part of the price we pay for damaging the ozone layer. Apart from this direct threat to humanity, there are other less obvious dangers. Increased UV-B radiation can, for instance, seriously damage aquatic ecosystems. Phytoplankton is the main source of oxygen in the biosphere, making it a key element in climate regulation. It, too, is sensitive to UV-B. Scientists have calculated that a 16% reduction in the level of ozone would result in a 5% loss of phytoplankton, which would lead in turn to an annual loss of around seven million tons of fish. This would be nothing short of catastrophic, as at least 30% of all animal proteins consumed by human beings come from the sea.

Which substances are responsible and what are they used for?

The five substances that do the most harm to the ozone layer are listed below, along with their uses:
- freons or CFCs
  (chlorofluorocarbons)
    - aerosols
    - refrigerators
    - air-conditioning
    - plastic foam
    - solvents, detergents
- HCFCs
  (hydrochlorofluorocarbons)
    - temporary replacement for CFCs, less harmful to the ozone layer
- halons or bromofluorocarbons
    - fire-extinguishers
- carbon tetrachloride
    - CFC production
- 1, 1, 1-trichlorethane
    - solvent
- methyl bromide
    - agricultural pesticides

The two faces of ozone

The ozone layer is a kind of gaseous veil around the earth with a very low density. Ozone molecules are made up of three oxygen atoms (O_3) and mainly form in the stratosphere, 10 to 50 kilometres above the earth's surface. The 'layer' is at its most dense at a height of around 25 kilometres. If it were subject to the same pressure that we find at ground level, the ozone layer would be barely three millimetres thick. Ozone molecules perform the vital task of absorbing the short-wavelength ultraviolet rays given off by the sun. In this way, the ozone layer protects the biosphere's inhabitants from skin cancer, blindness and genetic damage. Paradoxically, while ozone in the upper atmosphere forms a protective layer, the oxidising effects of the same gas at ground level are deadly to vegetation, construction materials and above all human health.

Source : Frank Morgan, Science Photo Library

Europe in action
International mobilisation

The international community has swung into action since 1985 in an attempt to halt the depletion of the ozone layer. In protocol after protocol, targets have become stricter and deadlines shorter. Europe has now virtually stopped consuming CFCs. But the battle has still not been won.

What's Europe doing?

International negotiations have been going on since 1985 to deal with the threat posed by damage to the ozone layer. Europe has been at the forefront of this process, which is only fair given our own significant contribution to the problem. The European Community accounted for 21% of global CFC consumption (and 35% of consumption by the developed countries) in 1992. These figures relate to consumption rather than emissions, but 'consumed' CFCs will more than likely find their way into the atmosphere once the devices containing them have been used or destroyed. A tough policy backed up by strenuous effort has led to a considerable reduction in emissions of these substances. The story is very different, however, when it comes to tackling the issue of methyl bromide. It is very much the Canadians and Americans who have taken the initiative in this case, with Europe unable so far to agree to progressive measures.

CFCs outlawed

The 1987 Montreal Protocol set out a precise timetable for progressively scaling back the production and consumption of CFCs and halons. Although scientists were still not absolutely certain about the mechanisms

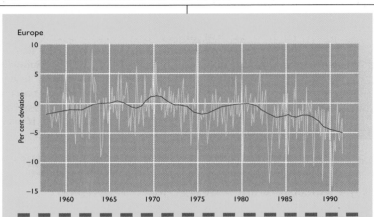

The average ozone concentration in the stratosphere above Europe fell by 6-7% between 1979 and 1994. A record ozone deficit of 45% over the northern hemisphere was recorded for the first time in the winter of 1995-1996. Bearing in mind that a 15% depletion in the ozone layer can translate into a 2% increase in the incidence of skin cancer, this poses a direct threat to human health.

Condroz, Belgium. Source: Walphot

and consequences of ozone depletion, the industrialised nations decided to err on the side of caution. The Montreal Protocol was the first international environmental treaty with a preventative character. After it was signed, however, new scientific evidence emerged, indicating that the measures adopted would not be enough. Consequently, the Protocol has been fundamentally revised on three occasions.

Watching the skies

A great many questions still have to be answered concerning the development of the ozone layer and the repercussions for the earth's ecosystems. The EU is putting up 30% of the finance needed for EASOE (European Arctic Stratospheric Ozone Experiment). EASOE was set up to observe the upper

Developments

The Good...   ...the Bad

- Use of CFCs restricted to a small number of applications (aerosols, refrigerants, solvents and foam plastic).
- New technologies allowing the replacement of CFCs.
- Industry has agreed to invest in this field.
- Pressure exerted on producers by a well-informed population.
- Limited transfer of new technologies between countries.
- Developing countries not being helped sufficiently to reduce their CFC consumption.
- Industrialised countries lack the will to ban the sale of ozone-harming substances.
- HCFCs difficult to replace in certain applications.

atmosphere and is the world's most important ozone research programme, currently employing 250 scientists in 17 countries.

Icebergs, Antartica.
Source : Benelux Press.

Taking responsibility

The European Commission acting at all levels

The EU uses the laws and regulations at its disposal to monitor and promote the steady reduction of substances harmful to the ozone layer. Its main tasks are as follows:

- limiting the amount of these substances that European companies are allowed to import ;
- monitoring production and imports ;
- requiring industrialists and Member States to supply the information it needs to fulfil its duties.

Towards the end of 1996, for instance, the Commission approved the launch of an eco-label for domestic refrigerators that do not contain ozone-harming substances and do not contribute to global warming.

International technology transfers

Huge sums have already been committed for investment in new technologies to help achieve concrete results at global level. It is every bit as important, however, that less developed countries also have rapid access to technologies and products that do not harm our precious ozone layer. The future of the stratosphere will depend to a large extent on the willingness of Europe and the other industrialised countries to put a stop to the production and sale of these substances beyond their own borders and to provide access to new technologies.

The ozone layer will continue to deteriorate until the turn of the century at least, and possibly beyond if the signatories to the Montreal Protocol do not apply the measures they have signed up to. There is an urgent need to restrict the damage as much as possible. Only a few solutions are available, the most realistic of which is to introduce measures as quickly as possible to restrict the use of substances that harm the ozone layer, such as HCFCs and methyl bromide. The European Union continues to the show the way as far as HCFCs are concerned, but not when it comes to methyl bromide. The Americans and Canadians are on track to eliminate this substance by 2001, while the European Union has so far failed to accept a complete ban even by 2010.

Why not stop sooner?

European Member States are currently introducing the legislation arising from the second revision of the Montreal Protocol (Copenhagen, 1992). Some have decided to ban the substances in question more quickly than Europe requires:

- The Swedish government ordered a total ban on HCFCs by 1995 rather than 2015 ;
- CFC and halon production had virtually ceased in Germany by 1993 instead of 1995 ;
- Halons were banned in Finland, the Netherlands and the UK in 1993 rather than 1994.

Take care especially behind the wheel!

The average European citizen used nearly a kilo of CFCs in 1986. How can we cut down? It's true that aerosols hardly contain any CFCs these days, but they have been replaced by derivatives like HCFCs, which still harm the ozone layer, although to a lesser extent. For that reason, it's better to use vaporisers instead of aerosol sprays and pots of paint instead of spray-paint. Another problem is caused by the disposal of old refrigerators which still contain CFCs. If this is done without special precautions, the CFCs can escape and attack the ozone layer. Ideally, old fridges should be dealt with by recycling centres - something that's beginning to happen in some countries. Air-conditioning systems also contain CFCs and steps have to be taken to stop them escaping into the atmosphere, especially during road accidents. Yet another reason for driving more carefully!

Aoos Valley, Greece.
Source : G.Heiss.

Facts and Trends
It's raining again...

Although we have been hearing about acid rain for over twenty years now, it remains a serious problem. It all starts when gases like sulphur dioxide (SO_2), nitrogen oxides (NO_X) and ammonia (NH_3) combine with water molecules in the air to form acids. When it rains, these acids enter our soil and water, changing their composition and threatening plants and animals with extinction. Most of the gases responsible for acidification are produced by power stations, manufacturing industry, road transport and intensive agriculture.

Nature under threat

It seemed at first that acid rain was less harmful to aquatic ecosystems than to those on land. Only now, however, is the impact of acidification making itself felt in certain regions of Europe. Acid conditions mean that heavy metals can dissolve more easily, and so acid rain has the devastating side-effect of increasing the concentration of these metals in water. Freshwater fish have been poisoned on a huge scale by dissolved aluminium from the soil flowing into lakes and rivers. Countless aquatic biotopes have been severely damaged in Scandinavia, and thousands of hectares of forest in Scandi-navia and Central Europe have also been acutely affected. In 1992, one tree out of every four in Europe was found to be losing its leaves at a rate of more than 25%, and 10% of them were discoloured. Although acid rain is not the only cause of these problems (the impression given in the 1980s), it is still the primary culprit. When we consider that a third of Europe's land area is covered in woodland and that forestry employs as many people as the car or chemical industry, it quickly becomes clear that damage to our trees is an economic issue, too.

Disfiguring monuments

Acid rain can harm a wide variety of materials, including stone, cement, paint, varnish, paper and textiles. That means it is slowly but surely damaging Europe's architectural heritage. And that's not all. Apart from acidification, sulphur dioxide, nitrogen oxides and ammonia also contribute to:
- global warming,
- ozone depletion,
- deteriorating air quality,
- eutrophication of surface waters and aquatic and terrestrial ecosystems.

What's to blame?

The most important sources of acidification are power stations, which were responsible for 64% of sulphur dioxide emissions in 1990, and road transport, which accounted for 50% of nitrogen oxide emissions in 1995 - a figure that continues to rise. Other culprits are industry, waste-processing plants, domestic heating, air transport (forecast to double between 1995 and 2000) and the ammonia produced by excessive fertiliser use and animal dung.

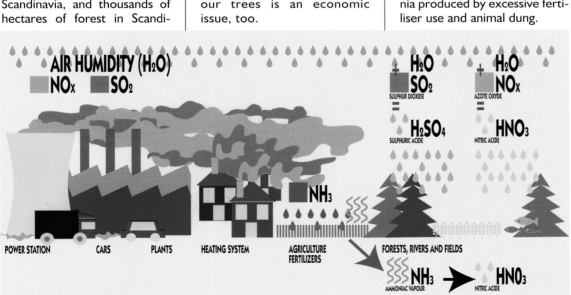

Sulphur dioxide (SO_2) and nitrogen oxides (NO_X) combine with water molecules in the atmosphere to form sulphuric and nitric acid. When these acids are deposited on the earth's surface, they change the composition of the surface waters and soil, seriously affecting the existing ecosystems. Ammonia (NH_3) is transformed into nitric acid in the soil rather than in the atmosphere.

Europe in action

Mobilisation

Europe is trying to halt the acidification process by establishing maximum rates or 'critical loads' for acidifying substances (primarily SO$_2$, NO$_x$ and NH$_3$) throughout its territory. Although significant progress has been made - in spite of limited resources - the target is unlikely to be met. Critical loads will be exceeded in many regions in 2005 and 2010 unless further action is taken very quickly.

Europe has built-up a whole arsenal of legislative measures and has signed numerous international agreements over the past twenty years in its attempts to win the battle against acidification.

- The 1979 Geneva convention on long-range transboundary air pollution led to targets for reducing nitrogen oxide (NO$_x$) emissions. A first protocol was adopted for sulphur dioxide (SO$_2$) in 1985 and a second in 1994.
- The EC Directive on air pollution from industrial plants introduced a series of measures aimed at the energy, metal, chemical, wood pulp and waste-processing industries. The most recent version of the Integrated Pollution Control Directive, or IPC Directive as it is known, adopts a fresh, integrated approach to tackling pollution, based on the use of the best available technology.
- The EC Directive on air pollution from large combustion plants is aimed primarily at power stations. The latest revised version will further tighten emission standards for SO$_2$ and NO$_x$.
- Several Directives on municipal and hazardous waste incineration have imposed emission limits for installations of this kind.
- The EC Directive on the sulphur content of certain liquid fuels fixes maximum sulphur levels for diesel. Similar measures exist or are planned for all fuel used in the transport sector (land, sea and air) and

Nitrogen oxide and sulphur dioxide emissions were substantially higher than their 'critical charges' in many regions of Europe in 1993. The situation is expected to improve significantly in certain areas by the year 2000, but other regions (Central, Northern and Eastern Europe) will continue to be badly affected for several years to come. Acidifying substances can travel thousands of kilometres in the atmosphere before they are finally deposited on the ground. That means some regions are suffering from other countries' emissions.
(NB: critical charges are expressed as chemical equivalents per hectare and per year. The results presented in this map do not take account of NH$_3$, as reliable data is not available).

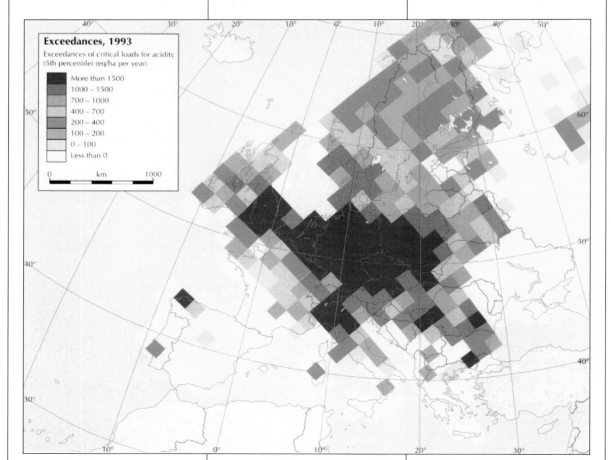

Exceedances, 1993

Exceedances of critical loads for acidity
(5th percentile) (eq/ha per year)

- More than 1500
- 1000 – 1500
- 700 – 1000
- 400 – 700
- 200 – 400
- 100 – 200
- 0 – 100
- Less than 0

0   km   1000

in heating and energy generation.

- The 'Auto Oil' programme, presented by the European Commission in 1996, sets out new, stricter standards for private cars (catalytic converters and more frequent inspections) and for fuel quality. The programme was developed in collaboration with car manufacturers and the oil industry.

- Europe has also adopted the following targets for the year 2000 as part of its Fifth Environmental Action Programme (5EAP):
  SO_2: 35% reduction compared to 1985 emission levels
  NO_x: 30% reduction compared to 1990 emission levels
  NH_3: targets vary from state to state, depending on the extent of the problem.
  Longer-term targets will be set shortly for the years 2005 and 2010.

Varying results

All Member States easily met the 1994 target of reducing sulphur emissions by 35%. The outlook is equally good for the year 2000, by which time a 50% reduction is to be achieved compared to 1985 levels. The rapid decline was due mainly to progress in the field of electricity generation. Increasing use of gas, lower sulphur content of fuel and new tax measures (differential fuel taxes based on sulphur content) have also made a positive contribution.

The situation for NO_x emissions, however, is much more worrying. We are nowhere near achieving the target of a 30% reduction by the year 2000. Private car use and road transport of goods are the main culprits, despite the introduction of catalytic converters. Steady growth in these areas has so far cancelled out the improvements achieved by the power generators and by industry.

Developments

The Good...   ...the Bad

- Catalytic converters.
- Road traffic restrictions.
- Reduction in the sulphur content of fuels.
- Progressive replacement of fuel oil with natural gas.
- Reduction in emissions from power stations and industry.
- Increasing transport of people.
- Increasing transport of goods.
- Poor performance of catalytic converters (especially when cold).
- Slow upgrading of car fleet (maximum 10% a year).
- Lack of new technology.
- Biofuels not competitively priced.

And little has yet been done to tackle NH_3 emissions. Several countries have completed an assessment of the current situation, but so far none of them have set effective limits. Despite a considerable reduction in acid emissions, the available data suggests that most of the targets set by the Fifth Environmental Action Programme will not be met unless additional measures are taken.

Southern France.
Source: Frank Spooner Pictures.

Taking responsibility

Role of Member States

Member States have a crucial part to play in ensuring that the critical loads set for acidifying substances are not exceeded. New measures will be needed to reduce emissions, especially those produced by manufacturing industry, power generation, agriculture and, above all, transport. The most significant progress in the coming years is likely to be made in Denmark, Germany and the Netherlands. So far, however, acid rain has barely affected the southern states (particularly Portugal and Greece) and so emissions of sulphur dioxide, nitrogen oxides and ammonia are all likely to continue rising in these countries for several more years.

Transport in the spotlight

The outlook is most negative in the field of transport, which continues to grow steadily. It is basically up to individual Member States to decide whether or not the problem is to be tackled effectively. Alternatives do exist. Emissions from cars, for example, can be reduced by promoting public transport and developing electric vehicles (provided that electricity generation is also subject to strict pollution controls). Preference should also be given to transport by rail or waterway rather than by road.

The fossil fuel burned by aircraft introduces significant quantities of nitrogen oxides and sulphur dioxide into the upper atmosphere. This is a cross-border problem that needs to be tackled at international level. Europe can impose maximum emission limits on aircraft, but fuel quality standards are set by the International Air Transport Association (IATA). The same goes for maritime transport, where fuel quality is fixed and policed by the International Maritime Organisation.

Better management of other human activities

Cars, air travel, heating, intensive agriculture and manufacturing all inevitably contribute to the acidification of the environment. European Directives and other administrative measures are intended to influence citizens' choices and to improve the environmental performance of European industry. They are also designed to encourage significant behavioural changes, including the more rational use of energy, production capacity and transport, and a more sustainable approach to agricultural production. For their part, citizens have to be persuaded by tax incentives and better infrastructure to use public transport, to cycle and to rediscover the simple pleasure of walking.

Monorail, London, UK. Source : Benelux Press.

Facts and Trends

Reach for your gas-masks!

t is a common misconception that air pollution simply disperses over time into the vastness of the atmosphere. Sadly, that is not the case. Some pollutants are trapped at low altitude and end up being deposited on the ground. Road traffic, the burning of fossil fuel and industrial activity all create air pollution that has a serious impact on our citizens' health and harms Europe's ecosystems. Surprisingly, all this damage is inflicted by substances that make up only 0.1% of the total atmosphere - pollution is actually the result of tiny local shifts in the concentration of gases. Although some improvement has been achieved, an immense amount still remains to be done.

Air pollution. Source: Gamma.

What do we mean by "air quality"?

Human beings need good quality air twenty-four hours a day in order to survive. In the modern world, however, economic activity, the burning of fossil fuels, waste incineration and intensive agriculture are generating ever-increasing amounts of pollution that damage not only our own health, but also that of plants, animals and habitats. It is even bringing about changes in the earth's climate. Our cities are threatened by low altitude smog, caused by a mixture of human activity (pollution) and natural factors (climatic and geo-graphical conditions). Far from being a strictly local problem, half of all the pollutants in the air were originally produced a considerable distance away.

Summer...

When the sun shines, the gases given off by car exhausts (NO_x and VOCs) combine to form ozone. Although the earth needs ozone in the upper atmosphere, the effects of the gas at low altitude are very harmful. The ozone concentrations experienced during summer smog often exceed the limits set by the World Health Organisation (WHO), damaging the health of over 100 million Europeans .

...and winter alike

Winter smog, meanwhile, is created when pollutants are trapped by the mass of cold air above our cities, causing them to build up (especially SO_2, NO_x and particles). The worst pollution tends to occur in the urban environment, where two thirds of Europe's people live. The WHO's air quality guidelines are broken at least once a year in three quarters of Europe's big cities. The primary culprit is the steady growth of car traffic.

Europe in action

Coherent approach towards air pollution

Air pollution has been one of Europe's main political concerns since the late 1970s. A series of Directives has been introduced to cut emissions of certain pollutants and to monitor their concentrations in the air. The thinking behind them has, however, been inconsistent and they have not been applied with equal vigour in all Member States. The most recent regulations are designed to tackle the problem of air pollution more coherently and effectively.

What is Europe doing?

In proportion to its size and population, Europe is one of the worst offenders when it comes to air pollution and climate change. The Commission has already launched a number of initiatives to correct this situation, focusing particularly on the following areas:

- protecting the ozone layer (by CFC reduction)
- reducing emissions of acidifying substances (SO_2 and NO_x)
- resisting climate change and reducing emissions of greenhouse gases (CO_2, CH_4 and N_2O)
- reducing the concentration of lead, asbestos, VOCs and ozone in the atmosphere.

A great deal of progress has already been made in tackling certain pollutants (SO_2, lead and CFCs).

New framework directive

Europe has decided that it can only guarantee equal protection for all its citizens if the monitoring and management of air quality is harmonised throughout its territory. It has therefore drafted a new framework directive which sets out a common strategy towards air quality, leaving it up to individual Member States to decide what specific measures they need to take.

In addition to protecting public health and safeguarding ecosystems, the directive has three

Road traffic, Milan. Source : Michael St Maur Sheil.

main aims:

1. To ensure the uniform evaluation of air quality.
2. To establish limits and warning thresholds for thirteen hazardous substances.
3. To tell the public which areas suffer from high air pollution and to notify them when safety limits have been breached.

Cleaner road vehicles.

A whole series of Directives has been aimed at motor vehicle emissions, as a result of which our cars, trucks and buses are already significantly

Origin and dangers of the main air pollutants

Pollutant	Principal origin (1990 figures)	Dangers
Ozone (O_3)	• formed from NO_x and VOC by the action of sunlight	• nose and throat irritations • headaches • pulmonary damage
Fine particles and heavy metals	• industrial emissions and exhaust gases	• irritation and damage of respiratory functions • occasional mutagenic and carcinogenic properties
Volatile organic compounds (VOC)	• road transport (36%) • use (25%)	• wide-ranging impact, from olfactory complaints to mutagenic and carcinogenic effects (benzene)
Carbon monoxide (CO)	• road transport (65%)	• affects tissue oxygenation
Nitrogen oxides (NO_x)	• road transport (51%)	• respiratory effects • inhibits plant growth • acid rain
Sulphur dioxide (SO_2)	• burning of fossil fuels (66%)	• exacerbates respiratory pathology • acid rain
Dioxins	• waste incineration • combustion plants	• probably carcinogenic. • probably attacks immune system and alters concentration of reproductive hormones.

cleaner than they used to be. Despite this progress, Europe's roads remain a steadily worsening source of pollution as traffic volumes continue to rise. It is hard to predict future developments, but there is little to suggest that the problem will diminish in the next few years. A great deal will depend on the 'Auto Oil' programme and the zeal with which Member States apply European regulations.

The latter focus on the following areas:
- fuel quality (lead and sulphur content),
- cleaner exhaust gases (catalytic converters),
- CO_2, CO, VOC, NO_x and particle emissions,
- regular vehicle inspections,
- research into new forms of propulsion and fuel.

North Yorkshire, UK. Source : Spectrum Color Library.

Developments

The Good...   ...the Bad

- Improved fuel quality.
- Use of catalytic converters, the performance of which is improving.
- Application of the directive on oil storage and distribution.
- Use of cleaner technologies in industry and transport.
- Application of the solvent directive (still under discussion).
- Use of water-based solvents.
- Growing road traffic.
- Delays in the adoption and application of directives.
- Increasing solvent use by industry.

Taking responsibility

Eula Saxe open air coal mine near Leipzig.
Source: Patrick Piel, Frank Spooner Picture.

Europe

It is all too often the case at European Union level that air pollution cannot be evaluated because of a lack of reliable and coherent data. We urgently need more effective measurement systems to identify the sources of air pollution and its impact on human health. Member States will have to act quickly and vigorously if they are to gather coherent, objective and comparable data on NO_x, VOC, dioxins and ozone emissions.

A register for industry

Directives aimed at industrial plants have successfully reduced emissions of certain pollutants in recent years. This trend is likely to continue with the promotion of very strict operating standards and promotes the use of the best available technologies. The Commission is also considering imposing an 'emissions register' which would oblige industry to keep a detailed record of substances believed to threaten public health and the environment. Such a register would be particularly useful when it comes to

keeping the public informed of air quality, one of Europe's key requirements in the field of communication and information access.

Cleaner petrol, cleaner cars

Directive 85/210 states that all cars built after 1993 must run on lead-free petrol. Each member state is required to ensure the availability and distribution of lead-free fuel within its territory. These regulations have undoubtedly done a great deal to reduce the health problems associated with lead, but lead-free petrol is still not a perfect solution, in that it contains more VOCs (and hence benzene) which are also harmful to human health. German legislation requires petrol storage installations and service stations to be fitted with devices to recover VOC fumes, which has had the effect of reducing hydrocarbon emissions by 13% between 1988 and 1992. Even better, the 1993 requirement that petrol-driven vehicles should be fitted with three-way catalytic converters has reduced VOC emissions by 75%. New technology which reduces

converter warm-up times is likely to further improve their performance.

Cities and citizens

Measures introduced in most European cities over the past twenty to thirty years have led to a reduction in emissions of certain pollutants. The main advances have been:
- the reduced sulphur content of fuels (coal and heating oil)
- increasing use of natural gas
- the cleaning of industrial emissions

On the other hand, despite the fitting of catalytic converters , it has so far proved impossible to cut NO_x emissions because of the steady growth in road use. Some countries have had to resort to a complete ban on motor vehicles in urban areas whenever climatic conditions encourage the formation of smog.

European citizens can make their own modest contribution to reducing urban pollution by opting for public transport instead of their cars and by choosing less toxic fuels like LPG or natural-gas central heating.

Facts and Trends
Tackling the waste mountain

Waste is a by-product of our way of life in the industrial countries. Its volume is growing all the time, to say nothing of its complexity or toxicity. In today's Europe, household waste is being generated at a rate of over one kilogram per person per day! The way we manage this waste is often outdated and represents a serious health and environmental hazard that can only be reduced by drastic changes in production methods and consumption habits.

Worrying increase

Around 80% of the waste produced by modern societies is agricultural, mining and industrial and 20% domestic. Most household waste consists of materials that can be recycled (paper, metal, plastic, organic matter) plus a few products considered as 'dangerous' (batteries, some medicines, paint, aerosols, etc.). The worrying increase in the volume of household waste is partly attributable to the flooding of the market with products with a short useful life and non-returnable packaging. Products of this kind currently account for nearly 40% of all domestic refuse.

Waste processing and its consequences

The two main ways of disposing of waste are landfilling (69% in 1990) and incineration (18% in 1990). Both methods have their health and environmental risks. Therefore, the problem of waste treatment is much more complex and should be dealt with by solutions ranging from waste separation at source through recycling, to landfilling of waste end-products. Waste prevention must be however the top priority option for any sound waste management policy. This global strategy is the subject of a specific European policy (see the following page).

Public concern about waste

Rightly or wrongly, the choice of a landfill site or the construction of an incinerator is often objected to by the local population. Citizens campaign more and more vigorously against the building of waste processing sites near their homes, a phenomenon sometimes referred to as the 'NIMBY' syndrome ('not in my back yard'). Therefore transparency and public information are essential conditions for public involvement in decisions in this field.

Clean technology and eco-products

At the end of the day, the problems caused by waste will only be solved by preventative measures, which reduce waste creation by taking action at the source. New products must be designed with a view to reducing waste throughout the lifecycle, from production and packaging to sale, use and subsequent recycling.

European waste production

Approximately 2 billion tons of waste are generated every year by the European Union. Europeans generated around 390 kg of domestic waste per person per year in 1992. The trend is still upward and waste processing has become an acute problem. A study of six European countries found over 55,000 sites contaminated by waste products.

	AIR	WATER	SOIL
LANDFILL	• CH_4 and CO_2 emissions (greenhouse gases) • Unpleasant smells	• Leaching of pesticides, organic compounds, cyanide, nitrates and heavy metals into substrata	• Use of space • Build-up of hazardous substances in the soil
INCINERATION	• Emits SO_2, NO_X, HCl, organic compounds, dioxins, heavy metals	• Fallout of hazardous substances into surface water	• Dumping of incinerator ashes and smoke-cleaning residues

Source : Eurostat.

Europe in action
Slow progress

The European Community has been trying to reduce waste generation and to improve its management for the past twenty years. Some Member States have also had waste management policies before 1975. Action in this area has, however, proved very difficult. What's more, although encouraging results have been achieved in the recycling of paper and glass, waste production has continued to rise steadily. It will increase by around 30% between 1985 and 2000. We are a long way from meeting that goal.

Strategy

Europe's strategy has been to encourage sustainable and ecologically sound waste management, which does not threaten public health or the environment. Five strategic guidelines have been defined to this end:
1. Prevention (minimisation).
2. Recovery (recycling and reuse).
3. Improving disposal conditions.
4. Regulation of the transport of waste.

Objectives

To put this strategy into practice, the Fifth Programme formulated a series of concrete objectives from which many are legal obligations set out in Community Directives:
- Drawing up waste management plans in each member state.
- Reducing dioxin emissions by 90% between 1985 and 2000.
- Stabilising waste production at the 1985 level by the year 2000.
- Recycling and reusing at least 50% of paper, glass and plastic by the year 2000.
- Banning the export of certain categories of waste with effect from 2000.

It cannot be denied however that the Community's achievements as regards these objectives are not satisfactory. Indeed, waste quantities, for instance, have on average continued to grow.

What's Europe doing?

European institutions have taken a number of steps. Amongst the most important are:

- The Waste framework Directive (1975) which requires Member States to take all necessary steps to prevent waste generation, to encourage reuse and to ensure that waste is disposed of in a way that does not harm human health or the environment.

- The Directive on hazardous waste which sets more stringent requirements for the handling of this type of waste.

- The Regulation on the supervision and control of transfrontier waste shipments which set out controls for the shipment of waste. The penalties for illegal trafficking are left to Member States' responsibility.

- The Directive on packaging and packaging waste, which sets targets for recovery and recycling and proposes that a marking scheme for packaging be set up. It also prescribes information and education programmes to alert consumers to the benefits of recyclable packaging.

- Community legislation also exist on batteries and accumulators, used oils, sewage sludge, PCBs and incineration of waste. Proposals on waste landfilling and end of life

Household Waste. Source : Oscar Poss, Spectrum Color Library.

vehicles are currently being discussed.

- Regulations on ecological labelling to reward products which have a less severe environmental impact during their production, sale, use and disposal ('clean products').

- Regulations on the supervision and control of transfrontier waste shipments which set out controls for the shipment of waste. The penalties for illegal trafficking are left to Member States' responsibility.

Common principles

Key principles in Europe's common strategy for better waste management are:

1. The prevention principle: we should limit waste production by taking action at the source.
2. The 'polluter pays' principle and, by the same logic, the "producer responsibility" principle: the cost of dealing with waste should be met by the person or body that produced it.
3. The precautionary principle: we should anticipate potential problems.
4. The proximity principle: waste products should be dealt with as close as possible to the source. (To which must be added the "self-sufficiency" principle, according to which the Community as a whole and Member States individually are encouraged to become self-sufficient in disposing of waste produced in the territory, rather than relying on the export of waste).

Plastic bottles awaiting recycling.
Source : Peter Ryan/Science Photo Library

Developments
The Good...   ...the Bad

- Development of clean technology and eco-products.
- Encouragement of citizens to sort and recycle waste and to choose products more carefully.
- Public opposition to landfilling.
- Taxes on packaging.
- Taxes on waste landfilling.
- Rising production and consumption.
- High cost of selective collection and sorting, making recycling economically unattractive.
- Lack of markets for certain recycled materials.
- Lack of internalisation of external costs.
- Complexity and diversity of the measures to be introduced.

Results

Although considerable advances have been made in recent years in waste management legislation, the translation of community regulations into national law has been very slow. Consequently, the most recently adopted regulations will only begin to bear fruit in several years' time.

Furthermore, in order to measure such results it is vital that Europe sets up a common programme to gather reliable and comparable data from the respective Member States. Differences in interpretation are currently preventing a clear overall impression of the production and processing of waste products across the European Union.

Taking responsibility

National plans

Under Community legislation, Member States are obliged to draw up waste management plans for waste in general, for hazardous waste and for packaging and packaging waste. In addition to and separate from this planning obligation, they are required to set up separate collection systems for certain batteries.

At the same time, a number of Member States already have in place their own systems for the collection and recycling of cars, electronic scrap, batteries and used tyres, and many of them make great effort to promote clean technology in manufacturing processes.

Member States are now responding to the pollution problems caused by lax waste management by drawing up integrated and sustainable management strategies. In practice, the following measures are promoted:

- Selective refuse collection and taxed bin bags.
- Introduction of deposit systems for returnable packaging.
- Promotion of clean technology.
- Involvement of industry in the recovery and recycling of their used products.
- Creation of markets for recycled products.

Industry must act

Industry has a crucial part to play when it comes to reducing the volume of waste, because it can take action at the source - during the design and manufacture of products. Industry also has to introduce collection and recycling systems for used products, as already exist in a number of countries for packaging, paper, batteries, tyres, used cars and trucks and electronic equipment.

Manufacturers should also do their best to use as few natural resources as possible and to produce a minimum amount of waste. Big companies have begun to minimise waste in industrial processes ('internalisation' as it is called) and to pursue the goal of 'zero waste, zero defect'. New cars, for instance, will soon be 100% recyclable - a principle that should be applied in other fields too.

Citizens should sort their rubbish and become more discerning consumers

Europe's citizens can also do a great deal when it comes to reducing waste. Their purchasing behaviour and the way they dispose of used products can have a very strong influence. We should all get into the habit of:

- Sorting our refuse and taking part in recycling and reuse programmes.
- Choosing durable products with a long useful life.
- Giving preference to recycled and recyclable products.
- Cutting down on packaging and reusing it.

390 kg of domestic waste per person per year in 1992.

Facts and Trends
A dangerous trend

Public awareness of the risks associated with waste management, particularly with hazardous waste, has risen sharply in the wake of major pollution incidents and proven damage to health. This in itself, however, is not enough to reverse current trends.

35 million tons of hazardous waste a year

Approximately 2% of the estimated 2 billion tons of waste generated in the European Union every year is classified as hazardous. Most of this waste has an industrial origin although there are elements of household waste such as certain paints, solvents, batteries and oils which are hazardous and should be separately collected from ordinary household waste to avoid harm to the environment being caused.

Industrial waste

Some industrial wastes can be hazardous, which complicates their disposal. Examples are:
- **Agricultural** wastes can contain pesticide residues.
- **Sludge** from dredging and purification plants often has

Every year, millions of tons of hazardous waste are shipped across the globe, often ending up in countries where disposal is cheapest but least secure. The general pattern is for wastes to move from the countries of the North to those of the South, and from the West to the East. Hazardous waste is also shipped back and forth within the European Union because of differences in taxation, processing expertise and the level of official supervision in the respective Member States.Source : Based on waste export data provided by individual countries to OECD.

high concentrations of heavy metals and organic compounds.
- **Building** wastes can contain asbestos and other hazardous substances.
- **Hospital** wastes include certain contaminated materials.

Thousands of contaminated sites

More than 55,000 sites contaminated by waste disposal have been identified in six European countries alone, but this inventory (Carrera and Robertiello, 1993) reveals the inconsistency of contaminated site's definition rather than their actual number. Nevertheless, almost half were found to be in a critical state, threatening public

health and groundwater quality in the vicinity of the site. Annual clean-up costs for the EU as a whole amount to a prohibitive ECU 1,000,000,000,000.

Radioactive waste

Every nuclear power station produces thousands of cubic metres of radioactive waste a year. Most of it is only slightly radioactive, but a small proportion, originating from the station core, is highly dangerous and has to be vitrified (encased in a solid block) before being buried deep in the earth's crust. It will remain active for centuries and the long-term repercussions of its presence are still far from clear. The recent case surrounding La Hague shows the potential risks involved in treatment of waste. The decommissioning of obsolete nuclear plants and the transport of radioactive waste also cause serious health and safety problems.

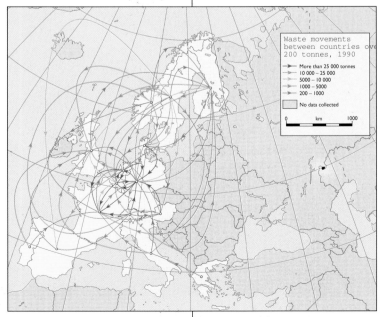

Waste movements between countries over 200 tonnes, 1990
- More than 25 000 tonnes
- 10 000 – 25 000
- 5000 – 10 000
- 1000 – 5000
- 200 – 1000
- No data collected

0   km   1000

Europe in action

Sustainable waste management - an ambitious goal

Although recycling has undoubtedly been a success, the progress it has achieved has largely been cancelled out by rapid growth in the volume of hazardous waste. Europe faces several major challenges in this area, not least the need to get to grips with the problems caused by hazardous waste. Measures have been proposed but it is likely to be many years before these bear fruit.

Several pieces of legislation have been introduced to deal with the problem of hazardous waste at European level. The main ones include:

- The **hazardous waste** directive which requires Member States to abide by certain rules for its collection, handling, recycling and treatment. This entails the regular inspection of companies that handle hazardous waste, introducing regulations to ensure that it is correctly packaged and labelled and drawing up emergency procedures.

Fly-tipped refrigerator,
South Glamorgan, Wales.
Source : Michael St Maur Sheil.

- The **incineration of hazardous waste** directive which sets out to prevent and minimise emissions.

- The regulation on the supervision and control of shipments within, into and out of the European Community has the aim to minimise waste movement. Under this regulation, exports of hazardous waste, whether for disposal or recovery, to non-OECD countries will be prohibited as of 1 January 1998. These regulations enshrine in Community law a number of international agreements on the movement of waste, including the Basle Convention.

A matter of definition

Before we can manage and regulate hazardous waste movements more effectively, we have to harmonise our definitions at European and international level. For the purpose of Community law, the term "waste" has been defined by the 1975 Waste Framework Directive, and a 1994 Council Decision defined what is hazardous and at the same time established the "Hazardous Waste List".

Radioactive waste

A joint seven-year action plan was adopted in 1992 for the period 1993-99. It focuses on the problems associated with radioactive waste and encourages Member States to co-operate in the field of:
- enhanced information for the public;
- permanent analysis of the situation (e.g. radioactivity levels);
- heightened safety efforts for the storage of radioactive waste.

Meanwhile, a directive on the monitoring and regulation of **radioactive waste shipments** defines the procedures to be followed during transportation.

Developments
The Good...   ...the Bad

- Selective collection and recycling programmes are enjoying growing success.
- European citizens and Member States are becoming increasingly aware of the need to avoid waste creation.
- Improved product design, clean technologies and the use of less hazardous materials could significantly reduce volumes of industrial and hazardous waste.
- Current trends suggest that the volume of hazardous waste will continue to grow between 1990 and 2000.

Anti-nuclear manifestation,
Dusseldorf, D.
Source : Benelux Press.

Taking responsibility

Reducing waste movements at international level

Adopting international rules to limit waste shipments is vital if we want to prevent the most hazardous waste products from being systematically shipped to the regions with the most lax environmental regimes. This issue was first addressed in 1989 by the Basle Convention on the "Control of Transboundary Movement of Hazardous Wastes and their disposal". The 116 signatories to the convention agreed that henceforth the exporter of the wastes in question was to be responsible for their proper treatment.

Cleaning the coast.
Source : Benelux Press

Source : Adam Hart-Davis/Science Photo Library.

Industry - immense potential

Experts believe that hazardous waste and toxic emissions can be cut by between 70 and 100% using better technology and rethinking product designs. Toxic compounds (CFC, chlorine, certain solvents, heavy metals), can be removed from certain products without altering their properties

Citizens are mobilising

Major accidents have shown all too clearly that the burial of hazardous waste can cause significant public health problems. Landfill disposal has a very poor image in the eyes of the public, who are objecting ever more vehemently against the creation of new sites. The same kind of opposition has been shown towards waste-processing and incineration plants, presenting decision-makers with serious difficulties.

Meanwhile, a significant section of the population has shown a strong commitment towards actively reducing waste by carefully choosing which products to use in the first place.

Facts and Trends
Noise and Smog

Towns are highly complex ecosystems whose environmental impact on the planet is increasing all the time. Europe has become highly urbanised in recent decades. Two out of three Europeans now live in towns, which account for only 1% of the continent's surface area.

Urban zones have a voracious appetite, however, that is out of all proportion to their size. On an average day, a European city with a million inhabitants consumes 320,000 tons of water, 2,000 tons of food and 11,500 tons of fossil fuel, while producing 300,000 tons of wastewater and 1,600 tons of solid waste. It goes without saying that there are countless interactions between town and environment. And the environmental problems already experienced by most European cities will get worse as their boundaries creep outwards and demand for mobility increases, further intensifying our dependence on the private car.

Blocked arteries and asphyxia

Vehicles used for road transport are public enemy number one across Europe when it comes to air pollution. Greater London alone is home to six million cars. Vehicles are responsible for congestion, stress and safety problems and they encroach on our public spaces. And most seriously they generate severe air and noise pollution.

Vehicle exhausts pump CO_2 into the atmosphere, contributing to global warming. They also produce HC particles, CO and NO_X. Road vehicles are a primary source of air pollution in our towns, in some areas far outstripping industry and households, where significant progress has been achieved (especially in Western Europe).

Modern factories produce more cleanly and have been moving towards the outskirts of urban areas. Meanwhile, atmospheric emissions have been reduced by increased use of natural gas as a heating fuel.

Green spaces serve a wide variety of purposes in urban areas. They are used for recreation and education and provide much-needed visual variety. Green areas fulfil other important roles too, such as improving air circulation, maintaining biodiversity, balancing humidity and capturing dust and gases. Maintaining and developing green spaces in towns is a key aspect of urban policy.

Unbearable noise

The percentage of citizens exposed to unacceptable noise levels (over 65 decibels) is steadily increasing, especially in the cities. The figure currently stands at 17% in the EU countries. Compared to Eastern Europe, however, EU citizens get off relatively lightly. Roughly 50% of the population in the East has to put up with this type of excessive noise pollution. Although aircraft noise poses a particular problem close to airports, even in these locations road traffic is the main culprit.

Ebb and flow

The pattern of water and waste flows clearly illustrates the burden towns place on the environment. Every day, town-dwellers consume 320 litres of drinking water each, even though only a tiny proportion (around 5%) is actually drunk or used in cooking. The dilapidated state of some water systems is also a problem, resulting in regular losses of between 30 and 50%. Some major cities don't have waste water treatment plants. As for solid waste, although progress has been made in the selective collection and recycling of refuse, the overall quantity continues to rise and the most common form of disposal is still landfill.

Cyclist in London. Source : David Townend, The Environmental Picture Library.

Europe in action
Directives and exchange of know-how

Just as populations are concentrated in towns, so too are environmental problems. We have already seen how air quality, noise and transport are intimately linked, and this is just one example. There are countless other connections like this in urban areas. For that reason, an integrated approach is needed if we want to pursue an effective urban environmental policy.

This need was reflected by the 1990 Green Paper on the Urban Environment. Three years later, the Sustainable Cities Project prepared recommendations for incorporating environmental issues at all levels of decision-making (EU, Member States, towns, etc.) and for taking them into account when considering other relevant fields like demographics and the economy.

This complexity means that there can be no single solution, but that each advance in a specific sector (water and air quality, for instance) helps improve the overall quality of the urban environment. Several EU policies have a direct impact in this respect by addressing a range of sensitive issues.

Pedestrian zone. Source : Frank Spooner Pictures.

Kurfürstendamm, Berlin. Source : Eye Ubiquitous.

More than anything, improving the environment requires the rethinking and effective application of policies towards planning, transport and the management of natural resources. In other words, it is not the tools as such that will provide the solution but the way they are used - the way elements contributing to the quality of urban life are integrated in the decision-making process (especially in terms of planning). This is not something that can be implemented at EU level. Policies like this have to be put into practice locally. With that in mind, the EU makes a significant contribution by encouraging towns to get together to compare experiences and to exchange information.

The EU and noise

As regards noise, European policy is concerned with assessing ambient noise levels, as well as introducing standards for vehicles, household appliances, tools, and so forth. In the Fifth Environmental Action Programme there are also general targets for the reduction of noise pollution:
- noise levels exceeding 85 dB to be banned;
- the percentage of the population exposed to noise levels above 65 dB at night must be reduced.

Developments
The Good...   ...the Bad

- Municipal regulations to cut air pollution have helped reduce emissions of harmful gases and particles.
- Noise-reduction measures have encouraged industry to perfect new, high-performance technologies, one achievement of which has been to produce quieter cars.
- Information concerning the urban environment is much more widely available to all relevant parties.
- Rising living standards and increased demand for consumer goods and mobility are cancelling out the positive effects of anti-pollution measures.
- The increasing number of cars and kilometres travelled also tends to neutralise these effects.
- Data on the urban environment remains fragmentary. An absence of information and differences in data-collection methods are too often the norm.
- The total quantity of household refuse continues to rise, despite advances in separated collection and recycling.
- The growing demand for water places a serious burden on water supply and replenishment.

Metro station, London. Source : Benelux Press.

Taking responsibility

All concerned

The goal of sustainable urban development is a shared one. However, many Member States, like the Netherlands, take the view that it is up to individual towns and municipalities to decide how to achieve it. This shows that real opportunities exist in the shape of decentralisation and the delegation of responsibility.

City networks

Cities are innovating and linking up with one another to create inter-urban networks. The European Sustainable Cities and Towns Campaign, for instance, brings together over 300 local authorities which have undertaken to develop local action plans for sustainability which will enable the Rio commitments to be met. The Car-Free Cities network has existed in Europe since 1994 and advocates forms of mobility that are more respectful of the environment and the needs of residents in the participating towns. It draws up examples of good practice, such as children and young people's councils and local democracy campaigns.

Towns are the key players in their own environmental policy,

which means that residents have to feel more involved, either individually or through committees and associations.

The growing number of public-private partnerships shows the many varied forms this general co-operation can take.

Effective town planning

It's one thing to know the level of air pollution at which certain people are likely to experience breathing difficulties, but quite another to transform this limit into a standard. European towns have found it very difficult to monitor these parameters, whether in the field of air, water, soil or noise. Taxes, tolls and permits offer partial solutions, but other mechanisms are needed too.

Town planning is an excellent tool for improving the urban environment. The ecological management of urban areas requires careful attention to the location and form of development of different types so as to minimise the need for motorised transport and to protect valuable natural and built environments, cleaning-up dilapidated areas,

pursuing an ambitious green-space policy and replacing inadequate infrastructure.

New models of transport

The planning of land use and transport must go hand in hand. Effective bus networks alone are not enough to solve the problems of urban mobility. Solutions are needed that offer a variety of choices. The keyword is integration: creating pedestrian zones, reducing the speed of car traffic, integrating the different modes of transport, developing safe and attractive cycle routes, reducing the availability of parking and developing other stimuli such as higher taxes on lone drivers.

Enhanced technology and improved management could strongly reduce raw material and waste flows. A number of interesting initiatives have been mounted in certain Northern European towns. Small in scale, many of these projects set out to reduce energy bills and hence to protect nature by promoting water purification, thermal insulation, a range of highly sophisticated procedures and the simple use of common sense.

Air pollution in Athens. Source : Frank Spooner Pictures.

FRESHWATER

MARINE AND COASTAL WATERS

ENVIRONMENTAL RISKS

SOIL

Facts and Trends
A complex and fragile system

The element of water is crucial to life on earth. Since the beginning of the 20th century, however, it has come under increasing threat. In a number of countries, including some in Europe, the quality and scale of water supplies is likely to be the focus of major tension and perhaps even conflict in the decades to come.

Limited reserves and excessive demand

Some 65% of our water supplies come from deep within the earth. They are pumped from subterranean aquifers containing limited reserves that only replenish themselves slowly - chiefly from rainwater percolating down from the surface. Water extraction rose by almost 35% between 1970 and 1985 and has shown no sign of slowing down more recently. The point has now been reached in an increasing number of regions where the natural replenishment of the water supply can no longer keep pace with demand. Water consumption has risen explosively as economic activity has expan-

ded. Industry accounts for 53% of total demand, agriculture for 26% and domestic consumption for 19%. Not only do these sectors swallow up vast amounts of our water resources, they also generate a whole range of pollutants that are affecting the quality of surface water (rivers, lakes, etc.) before filtering down into the substrata. Annual water consumption in Europe varies between 200 and 1,000 cubic metres per head of the population, depending on the level of economic development. Incidentally, it is not the countries with the most water (basically those in the North) which consume the most or try hardest to conserve supplies. Irrigation is growing constantly in the countries of the South.

From source to ocean

Water is adversely affected by the presence of human beings even before it begins to form rivers. Industrial production, animal husbandry, arable farming, accidental discharges and domestic cleaning all release a range of pollutants into the soil, many of which gradually filter their way down into the groundwater. The contaminated water then rises and begins its slow journey to the sea. On the way, it picks up untreated industrial residues and wastewater containing organic matter and phosphates from built-up areas. Rainwater runs off roads and farmland into the river, carrying with it nitrates, pesticides, hydrocarbons, atmospheric acid deposits and other everyday residues. Meanwhile, certain species of fish are disappearing and others are being confined upstream of dams or behind the thermal barrier created by power station discharges. Many plants are being suffocated by a lack of oxygen, allowing others to proliferate in their place at the expense of animal life. And when the river finally makes it to the sea, it promptly deposits the pollutants it has carried downstream.

Insidious threat

Although industry is the single greatest source of pollution, it is not viewed by environmentalists as the most challenging adversary. After all, there are various ways of encouraging industrialists to manage their water resources more effectively. It is much more difficult to curb the thousands of millions of micro-pollutants introduced by the spreading of fertiliser and manure, by pesticide and biocide use and by leaks from the millions of underground tanks used to store heating oil.

River Ticino, Switzerland.
Source : Michael St Maur Sheil.

Europe in action
A global approach to the aquatic ecosystem

he fight against water pollution was one of the very first policies to be taken in hand by Europe. This early response resulted in concrete actions which continue to bear fruit today. It has also been translated into educational programmes designed, in the light of earlier errors, to ensure that European action is more effective and coherent.

Developing an integrated approach

The European authorities responded to the alarming deterioration in the continent's water resources back in 1973, close on the heels of international mobilisation to tackle the pollution of the Rhine. A score of directives designed to protect aquatic ecosystems have since been issued, focusing on specific areas like bathing water, drinking water, groundwater and fish and shellfish water. The main intention of these measures has been to set European quality standards for water intended for specific human needs. The Drinking Water Directive, for instance, sets limit values for a large number of parameters, thus providing safety for the consumer. As for bathing water, the Directive

aims at ensuring a safe and healthy quality of the water by primarily setting standards for faecal pollutants. Although the application of these measures in the different Member States has undoubtedly raised awareness and produced some valuable initiatives, these have not been enough to offset the growing pressure exerted on water quality by demographic development and intensified economic activity. Earlier European strategy did not take enough account of either the diversity of the individual situations encountered or the specific priorities of the different regions and their aquatic ecosystems: precipitation, evaporation, catchment, river regulation, effluents, etc. What was needed was an integrated approach - one of the priority objectives of the Fifth Programme and the Edinburgh Summit in December 1992. For the future, preparations are underway for a

new European 'Framework Directive' which requires integrated water management planning on a river-basin basis and sets common rules to ensure comparability of effort and results.

The integrated approach of the Framework Water Directive

Unlike previous water legislation, the Framework Water Directive will cover both surface water and groundwater, as well as estuaries and coastal waters, in recognition of the natural interaction between surface waters and groundwaters in terms of quality and quantity. One of the innovations of this directive will be that rivers and lakes will need to be managed by river basin - the natural geographic and hydrological unit - instead of according to administrative or political boundaries. The river basin management plans will have to include an analysis of the river basin's characteristics, a review of the impact of human activity on the ecological status of waters in the basin and an economic analysis of water use in the district. Central to each river basin management plan will then be the requirement of each

The combined approach

The Framework Water Directive aims at achieving "good status" for all waters (groundwater and surface water) by 2010. To that end, a combined approach is foreseen :

• by setting emission limit values for all discharges and other relevant sources of pollution, such as agriculture, urban domestic waste water and industrial waste water, and

• by setting water quality standards to ensure that those controlled discharges and other relevant sources of pollution will not adversely affect the water quality and result in a good status of the water.

Member State to establish a programme addressing all the measures which need to be taken within its territory to ensure that all waters in the river basin achieve good water status by 2010.

Precise targeting

Other European goals in terms of water quality are set out in a number of texts, such as:

- The Drinking Water Directive sets quality standards for water destined for human consumption;
- The Urban Waste-Water Treatment Directive sets out the minimum conditions for the collection, treatment and discharge of domestic effluents (including comparable industrial waste);
- The Nitrates Directive is intended to reduce and prevent pollution caused by the storage and use of nitrate fertilisers in agriculture;
- The Bathing Water Directive combines environmental and public health concerns. On the basis of specific quality monitoring programmes established and carried out by the Member States, information is given by the Member States and the Commission to the public at large;
- An Action Programme for integrated groundwater management, currently being prepared, will tie together the basic measures enabling each member state to shape its own policy, while bearing in mind the common objectives and the overall group of shared 'enemies' that threaten the aquatic ecosystem. The action

Developments

The Good...   ...the Bad

- Major treatment projects have already been set up by the Member States.
- Leading industries have given the go-ahead for substantial investments to treat their wastewater.
- There is growing interest in integrated river management, such as river contracts and the joint cleaning up of the Rhine.
- Considerable advances have been made in the efficiency and effectiveness of water-treatment technologies.
- The policy of increasing prices and imposing taxes is clearly helping to raise awareness.
- Farmers are gradually recognising the impact of their activities on water quality.
- The amount of drinking water extracted is growing all the time, primarily because of the irrigation needs of intensive agriculture.
- Although significant advances have been made, these are not enough to offset the increase in new sources of pollution.
- The development of new agricultural policies and methods is likely to increase the amount of pollution caused by fertilisers and more active pesticides (effective at weaker concentrations, but also highly toxic).

programmes are focused on groundwater in the countryside and thus, in particular, affect agricultural practices.

The right price to reduce consumption

Few measures at European level have been specifically targeted at reducing domestic consumption. By contrast, Europe's support for products with a low environmental impact sets out to do just that, in this case by awarding eco-labels. By clearly informing consumers of the ecological benefits (such as water-conservation) offered by certain products on the market, the EU is giving them a concrete way of intervening in the field.

Meanwhile, Member States could help focus attention on the true economic value of water by ensuring that the true cost of treatment and purification is reflected in its sale price.

Lake Balaton, near Czopak.
Source : Spectrum Color Library.

Taking responsibility

Honest broker

The pollution of our rivers clearly shows that we urgently need a policy capable of addressing the management of water resources in their entirety. At the same time, it reveals just how complex the issue can be. To tackle this complexity, three sorts of action are envisaged at European level:

- Encouraging Member States to take stock of the situation and to identify sources of pollution;
- Defining concrete and realistic objectives in consultation with individual states;
- Setting up integrated programmes to achieve these objectives, in collaboration with all relevant parties.

Shared Responsibility

After adoption of legislation and action programmes on the EU level, Member States have to transpose and implement them correctly to achieve the environmental objectives. The EU provides information to raise citizens' awareness in environmental matters and funds to help Member States or NGO's on specific projects. It is this combination of different levels of action - legislation, implementation, citizens' awareness - that can lead to an actual improvement in water quality and sustainable management of water resources.

Clean technology firmly established

Not only was industry the first polluter to be identified, it was also the first to respond to the pressure exerted by European regulations, producing a significant improvement in water quality as a result. Faced with ever-more rigorous standards and steadily rising purification costs, companies are nowadays turning to new production techniques that use less water and are less polluting. Little by little, new environmental production standards like ISO 14001 or EMAS are gaining ground. The main purpose of these schemes is to persuade industry to start seeing the environment as a resource that is every bit as important as labour or capital.

Local government - keeping the public informed

Local authorities will be the first to experience the social and economic impact of the new policies on water. It will be

Source : Mercay, WWF.

up to them to explain to citizens why the price of water had to be adjusted and why investment is needed in water collection and purification. They will also be responsible for local testing. In other words, local government will have to raise awareness, inform, educate and explain in such a way that citizens stop looking on water simply as a natural way of transporting effluent to the nearest river, which is then transformed into a natural sewer.

More responsible farming

The intensive agriculture that has grown up in Europe is the main source of the nitrates and pesticides that find their way into our groundwater and surface water. Consequently, farmers will have to accept their share of the effort needed to preserve our water resources by controlling fertiliser use more effectively and preferring less toxic products and irrigation methods that use less water. Agriculturists in several countries have already committed themselves to concrete promotion of farming methods that are less harmful to the environment. These efforts need to be reinforced and above all to be applied more widely.

Demanding consumers

Every summer, Europe's citizens spray their gardens with 17 cubic metres of water per square metre. We use 200 litres every time we wash our cars and 100 litres to wash every five kilos of cloths. Everyday domestic consumption may be relatively modest compared to industrial demand (bear in mind it takes 25 litres of water to brew one litre of beer!), but citizens can still do their bit by paying more attention to our water resources. We can do this by saving water at home, buying washing-machines and dishwashers that consume less water, choosing cleaning and washing products that are less polluting and can be used in smaller quantities and by making better use of rainwater.

Facts and Trends

Europe's coast : 89,000 km of frontline

The coastal zone is the interface between land and sea, between freshwater and saltwater. It is here, without any doubt, that human beings and their activities have left their most visible imprint on our planet. These effects are all the more difficult to address, because they are the end-result of every imaginable type of pollution, flowing from a countless range of outlets.

The 13 EU Member States with access to the sea share a total coastline of around 89,000 km. Some 68 million of Europe's 360 million people live on this narrow strip of land, in concentrations varying from 3% in Belgium to 70% in Denmark. These figures are subject to extreme seasonal variations, which is one of the factors that make the coastal zone so sensitive.

Urbanisation, manufacturing, harbour activities, fishing, naval bases, tourism and leisure are the primary culprits behind the accelerating deterioration of our coastal ecosystems - the disappearance of undeveloped areas, declining biodiversity, water pollution, spoiled landscapes and the infiltration of saltwater into overexploited freshwater layers.

And as if these problems weren't enough, we also have to contend with the threat of a rising sea level and the marine disruption caused by climate change.

More people than ever are attracted to the coasts for recreation and holidays. But coasts also have another role as the final outlet for pollution, much of it generated far inland.

Virtually all the materials carried in suspension by our rivers and ejected into the sea are deposited at the coast, urban and industrial pollution or nitrates and pesticides that have leached into the soil or the deposit of atmospheric pollution.

The repercussions for the environment and for human health are numerous, complex and very difficult to evaluate in the long term. Pollutants, for instance, often re-emerge from coastal sediment several years later.

A precious habit being nibbled away

The coastal zone forms an irreplaceable breeding ground and habitat for plants and wildlife. Eight out of every 40 habitats rated as essential to survival and a third of all wetlands are located on the coast. The same strip also contains breeding and growing areas for most of the fish and shellfish species that end up on our plates.

These facts illustrate the scale of the problems sparked by human activities in these coastal regions, where entire chunks of these precious habitats have been sacrificed in recent years in the name of urbanisation, industry, tourism and fishing.

Suffocating the sea

The most dangerous pollutants threatening our coasts -often worse even than heavy metals, chemicals or hydrocarbons - are nutrients, which come mainly from fertilisers and urban refuse. These nutrients can cause excessive growth of plants, e.g. algae. Such masses of algae may physically leave no space for other forms of life in the water, as well as, -on their decomposition, - deplete the water of oxygen, suffocating the surrounding ecosystem. At the same time, they gradually destroy the coast's attraction to tourists.

Assailed from all sides

1. Overexploitation of local resources
2. Pollutant discharges
3. Heat discharges
4. Disturbance of the sea-bed
5. Disappearance of natural habitats
6. Sediment accumulation
7. Organic pollution
8. Unlicensed gas discharges
9. Solid waste dumping
10. Overexploitation of certain species

Europe in action

Careful co-ordination required

The greatest obstacle to protecting the coastal and marine environment is the huge variety of users and other interested parties at regional, national and international level. Industry, property-developers, fishermen, hoteliers, tourists, local authorities, environmental groups, researchers, transport firms and sports enthusiasts are all keen to defend their position on the coast. Each interest group is busily lobbying political decision-makers.

The result has been a multitude of decisions and initiatives which, though sometimes highly beneficial in local terms, often do little more than shift the problem to some other region. In some cases, they even create brand new problems at the same spot.

A raft of initiatives

The EU has drawn up and applied an impressive series of measures. The first of these dates from 1973 and relates to the protection of coastal zones. The Fifth Programme, which argued in 1993 for the formulation of a common strategy for integrated coastline management.

Highlights of the intervening period include several international conventions such as the Helsinki Convention on the protection of the Baltic marine environment (1974), the Oslo (1974) and Paris Conventions (1978) on the protection of the Northeast Atlantic, the Barcelona Convention on the protection of the Mediterranean and a series of conferences on protecting the North Sea. Not to mention directives on the quality of fish and shellfish water, the conservation of wild birds, the quality of bathing water, environmental impact studies, the cleaning up of waste urban waters, conservation of flora and fauna and nitrates. If we add in all the charters, joint declarations and recommendations,

we end up with almost thirty major European initiatives which have attempted to halt the damage to the coastal and marine environment. A great many financial instruments have also been created to support these efforts.

Although the progress achieved has failed to live up to the amount of energy expended, these efforts have borne fruit in several fields. The quality of bathing water has improved at many locations and the North Sea states have cut their phosphorus and heavy metal discharges by half.

At the same time, many national and local programmes have significantly improved the coastal and marine environment and helped recreate a natural habitat.

Getting the measure of the problem

It is incredibly difficult to come up with a precise evaluation of

Europe is surrounded by nine sea basins. Source : Stock Imagery.

any improvements or setbacks in the overall health of our coastal and marine environment. And it is just as hard to identify the real heroes and villains when it comes to local, regional and national management. We don't have reliable indicators for the state of our coastal waters, making it risky to attempt a diagnosis. One of Europe's main priorities is to give itself the proper tools to measure and evaluate its coastal and marine ecosystems.

Many instruments without an orchestra

Over the past 20 years, public and private bodies all over Europe have devoted themselves to restoring marine and coastal ecosystems. They have done so by launching specific programmes and actions with concrete, often local objectives - protecting plants and wildlife, reducing the discharge of specific pollutants, raising public awareness and drafting clearly targeted plans.

A well known example is the Blue Flag for the best environmentally managed beaches. This campaign has ensured public awareness for environmental issues, and in particular on the delicate ecological balance of the coastal strip.

Although some good has been achieved, we lack the necessary co-ordination between this plethora of individual initiatives.

The problem does not lie in the instruments themselves, but in the way they are orchestrated. To address this problem, Europe set up a demonstration programme in 1996, based on 20 carefully selected coastal zones. The aim of the project is to improve co-operation between all the individuals and bodies involved in coastal protection between now and 1999. It will do so by enhancing

Developments

The Good...   ...the Bad

- Bathing water quality has become a key issue for tourists.
- Successfully restored dunes and the rescue of threatened animal species demonstrate the potential effectiveness of what are often isolated and localised rehabilitation initiatives.
- Vital investment is taking place in industrial and urban waste processing.
- Awareness of these issues is now widespread in Europe and continues to rise.
- Once again, the absence of reliable and comparable data is undermining the effectiveness of controls.
- Many local initiatives still fail to take account of the repercussions on neighbouring ecosystems.
- Effective criteria have yet to be formulated for a better balance between town planing, environmental protection and the exploitation of natural resources.
- Too many countries outside Europe still have to be persuaded that these measures are truly necessary.

the distribution and management of data concerning the whole of Europe's 89,000 km of coastline.

Dumping of dredged contaminated mud adds harmful substances (such as heavy metals) to the marine environment. Source : Michael St Maur Sheil.

Taking responsibility

Sharing responsibility for the sea

The ecological quality of our coastal and marine zones can't be improved through legislation alone at European level, and even less so at national and regional level. The state of the Mediterranean or Baltic, for instance, is determined by the environmental policies of all the surrounding states. The health of Europe's coastal zones depends very strongly on the conduct of all the people who are active there, in sectors like shipping, fishing and the offshore industry. These are the currents and tides that truly determine the dilution and spread of any pollution. That's why Europe takes an active part in the international debate to persuade less committed countries to join it on its mission.

Clear vision for effective action

Europe has gone a long way towards deciding what ought to be done. Our next task is to find ways of putting these decisions into practice. The demonstration programme will be a vital tool in this process. By applying the most effective strategies, we will gradually restore the ecological balance of our marine and coastal zones, thereby ensuring sustainable development in the future. The creation of reliable and uniform evaluation tools will greatly enhance the co-ordination of all the parties whose decision-making has an impact on the way these ecosystems evolve. Meanwhile, reliable data-banks and effective instruments for data exchange and comparison will give the EU the information it needs to ensure that its Member States apply the agreed polices and instruments effectively. They will also enable it to assert its rights in negotiations with third countries involved in these complex issues.

Local initiatives: getting away from self-interest

It is generally understood nowadays that the economic future of our marine and coastal regions is closely bound up with the quality of their environment. As we have seen, though, efforts to safeguard this quality - improving bathing water, for instance, or saving a particular species of fish - do not always mean that the people concerned are willing to take part in an overall approach to environmental protection. For that reason, many local initiatives, usually taken with the best intentions in the world, have ended up harming the general interest of the fragile and vulnerable zones which border our coasts. Too often, measures to reduce one type of industrial pollution have simply allowed other problems to become established.

Greater professionalism and responsibility at sea

International marine transport is clearly implicated in the problem of marine and coastal pollution. The huge oil-slicks that have devastated parts of the European coastline over the past 20 years are simply the most spectacular illustration of this phenomenon. Emptying and cleaning tanks offshore, unlicensed dumping of waste and toxic products and intensive fishing all testify to the fact that many people see the ocean as something that is there to be used. And that when it comes to waste products and pollution, out of sight is out of mind. Responsibility often lies with badly trained or even untrained crews operating poorly maintained ships under flags of convenience. Europe has already acted (introducing navigation corridors, emergency systems, etc.) but the situation can only really be dealt with at international level, through tighter controls and stricter and properly enforced international rules.

Outflow from chemical plant, West Hartlepool, UK. Source : Michael St Maur Sheil.

Facts and Trends
Environmental risks and threats to society from natural and technological disasters

Practical experience indicates clearly the environmental risks and the threats that a modern society is facing. Natural disasters have had serious effects on the whole society in many European countries. Fires pose a substantial threat and the technological risks are growing. The protection of persons, environment and property from such risks is a general obligation for governments. The challenges for Civil Protection are therefore considerable.

Risks and threats

In recent years there is recognition of the necessity to accept the existence of a more extensive scope for Civil Protection. Naturally, the global development and the vulnerability or sensitivity of modern society is the background to this. Even if extensive integration within modern societies, including economic and technological development, has increased the ability to withstand and deal with difficult situations, modern development still involves increased risks. Accidents that have not been foreseeable or situations where sufficient preparedness measures have not been undertaken will occur. In the words of Aristotle it is likely that something unlikely will occur.

Disasters

The incidents in Europe affecting the environment seriously are well known for instance those involving the tankers Amoco Cadiz (230.000 tons of oil), Aegean Sea, Braer and Sea Empress, the Basel chemical accident with its consequences for the Rhine, the release of a chemical cloud containing dioxins at Seveso and the Chernobyl accident. Some examples of serious natural and technolo-gical disasters and their effects, other than environmental damage, are to be found in the table. Civil Protection has to be prepared for different types of serious emergencies.

Demands on Civil Protection

Most Member States within the framework of their Civil Protection are redefining their assessments of the environmental risks and accidental threats, or have already done so. The requirements on Civil Protection are being adjusted to meet and correspond to these risks and threats. There is also a general demand to make the public services more efficient by the best possible use of available resources in society.

Natural and technological disasters in the EU

1953 earthquakes in Ionian islands Greece, 455 dead, 4.400 injured, 27.700 buildings damaged
1963 landslide and flooding in Vaiont-Longarone, Italy, 1.759 dead
1976 volcano eruption of the Soufrière, Guadeloupe, 70.000 evacuated
1980 earthquakes in Campania/Basilicata, Italy, 2.739 dead, 8.816 injured, 334.000 homeless

1953 tidal wave and flooding, Zeeland, Netherlands, 2.000 dead, 300.000 affected
1954 avalanche, Vorarlberg, Austria, 125 dead
1959 dam breakage (Malpasset dam), Fréjus, France, 421 dead
1962 tidal wave and floods, Hamburg, Germany, 400 dead, more than 100.000 affected
1962 flooding in Barcelona, Spain, 500 dead
1967 flooding due to rainstorm, Lisbon, Portugal, 500 dead, landslides, infrastructure destroyed
1990 storms in Belgium, 19 dead

1967 department store fire (L'Innovation), Brussels, Belgium, 325 dead
1973 hotel fire, Copenhagen, Denmark, 35 dead
1981 fire in a bar, Ireland, 48 dead, 214 injured
1985 forest fires, north of the Tejo and south of Douro river, Portugal, 14 dead
1990 ferry fire (Scandinavian Star), off Sweden, 158 dead, 30 injured

1961 railway accident, Harmelen, Netherlands, 95 dead
1976 explosion and fire in a chemical installation, Flixborough, United Kingdom, 28 dead
1978 explosion of a gas tank truck, San Carlos de la Rápida (Tarragona), Spain, 216 dead, several hundreds wounded
1985 release of oil during loading in the Port of Naples, Italy, 7 dead, 19 wounded, 2.300 evacuated
1987 explosion of road tanker holding 36.000 l of gasoline, Herborn, Germany, 5 dead, 38 injured.
1992 plane crash into an Amsterdam block of flats, Netherlands, more than 50 dead
1994 ferry sinking (Estonia), off Finland, 865 dead.

* environmental risks and threats to modern society are growing
* Civil Protection has considerable increasing challenges

Chernobyl site after the accident. Source : Frank Spooner Pictures.

Europe in action
A new concept for facing the risks

The Community has taken significant action in response to the serious incidents that have occurred but also to improve preparedness. Programmes for promoting and supporting the ability of Member States in respect to Civil Protection policies have been introduced. Further actions are for instance pilot projects to develop better technology for emergencies. In the area of the control of major-accident hazards involving dangerous substances, Community legislation has been introduced. After the Chernobyl accident the Community has undertaken significant action to prevent similar disasters and improve the emergency preparedness and response measures but has also assisted in improving the safety of Soviet-built reactors.

Civil Protection

European co-operation in Civil Protection has been developing since 1985. The aim has been to support and promote action by Member States. The basic objectives are:

• To encourage and offer guidance to national, regional and local efforts in the field of disaster prevention, to help in the training of Civil Protection personnel and to offer assistance in the event of a disaster. A variety of actions provide measures to achieve this objective such as exchange of experts, workshops for exchange of experience and pilot projects.

• To set up a permanent framework for efficient and rapid co-operation between Member States in the event of an emergency.

Regular simulation exercises involving different Member States are conducted with the support of the Commission to test the effectiveness of emergency procedures using different realistic scenarios.

Much attention is devoted within Community cooperation on Civil Protection to information of the public in relation to accidents as well as training of the public on appropriate action to be taken. As many countries have involvement of volunteers in Civil Protection, these issues are also subject to Community cooperation. To facilitate action by the public in case of an accident, a single emergency number 112 has been introduced for getting necessary assistance from the Civil Protection services in all Member States.

Spills at Sea

A Community action plan allows Member States to respond more effectively to marine pollution incidents

The effectiveness of any evacuation plan has to be tested using simulated emergencies...
Source : EUR 13258

involving spills at sea of hydrocarbons or other harmful substances. The programme also creates the conditions for mutual assistance and effective co-operation and provides:

• A joint information system ensuring that national emergency teams have access to current detailed information on response capabilities, properties and behaviour of hydrocarbons etc.

• A training programme which gives national governments the qualified personnel required to respond to incidents and at the same time fosters a spirit of co-operation between Member States

• Pilot projects to develop better anti-pollution technology.

The Commission and national governments have been involved and co-operated in the response to a number of Marine pollution tanker incidents, including the recent Sea Empress accident off the Welsh coast in 1996, the wreckage of the Braer in the Shetlands in 1993 and the grounding and fire on the Aegean Sea in La Coruna in 1992.

Major-Accident Hazards involving Dangerous Substances

For hazardous, high-risk industrial activities previous legislation tended to focus on the protection of workers, the quality of manufactured products and standards for air and water pollution. The aim was to a great extent to safeguard normal operation. The 1982 Council Directive (SEVESO I) is concerned with the prevention of, preparedness for and response to major accidents involving dangerous substances. Following a fundamental review a new Directive (SEVESO II) has entered into force in February 1997.

The new Directive builds upon the existing Directive, but simplifies the scope and adds new requirements related to safety management systems, land-use planning, emergency planning, information to the public and inspection by the national public authorities. The Directive is applicable to establishments, which are defined as the whole area under the control of an operator where dangerous substances over certain threshold levels are present in one or more installations, including common or related infrastructures or activities.

The general obligation in the Directive is that an operator must take all necessary measures to prevent major accidents and, in case of such an accident, to limit its consequences and to be able to prove, at any time, that he has taken all these measures. All operators are obliged to have a major-accident prevention policy. For establishments in which dangerous substances are present in quantities above a higher threshold level there are more requirements such as to produce a safety report that has to be examined by the competent authorities and that must demonstrate all measures undertaken.

The SEVESO II Directive also contains a requirement for Member States to report to the Commission all accidents and to provide a more detailed analysis of an accident in a report. The accident information is gathered in a Major-Accident Reporting System (MARS) which has been esta-

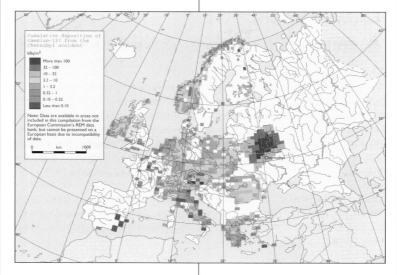

Cumulative deposition in Europe of Cs-137 from the Chernobyl accident.
Source : De Cort et al, 1990.

blished in the Major Accident Hazard Bureau (MAHB) at the Joint Research Centre (JRC) in Ispra, Italy.

Radiological Emergencies

The 1957 Euratom Treaty, which created the European Atomic Energy Community, set out to 'establish safety conditions that will reduce the threat to citizens' lives and health'. A directive was duly introduced in 1959 to protect workers and the population at large from the dangers to health resulting from ionising radiation.

The European Community's immediate response to the Chernobyl accident in 1986 was to take steps to protect its citizens from the consequences of the accident. It also re-examined its procedures for preventing similar disasters in its own territory and reviewed and introduced new measures to be carried out if such an incident did actually occur.

Throughout the process of political and economical reform in the former Soviet Union, the European Community has actively helped the authorities in the Ukraine,

Belarus and the Russian Federation to deal with the aftermath of the Chernobyl accident. Its main focus has been on improving the safety of Soviet-built reactors in Eastern Europe, permanently sealing off the Chernobyl plant and providing direct aid to the victims of the accident.

- Civil Protection programmes for promotion and supporting Member States are implemented
- Community support actions are conducted to deal with spills at sea
- All necessary accident prevention and mitigation measures are required at industrial establishments dealing with dangerous substances
- Any citizen in Europe can in an emergency call the one single number for assistance 112

Taking responsibility
Development to cover the new challenges

The authorities in each Member States are responsible for the conduct of civil protection within its territory. In recent years the use of risk assessment as a basis for undertaking both preventive and preparedness measures has been introduced and come into general practice. However, environmental risks and threats to society also call for continued efforts to develop and adapt resources to cover new requirements.

Action Programme

Within the Community Actions Programme on Civil Protection, contributing to the protection of persons, environment and property in the event of a natural or technological disaster, a rolling plan will be adopted with the intention of supporting and supplementing Member States' efforts and their actions on national, regional and local levels. The aim will also be to facilitate Civil Protection cooperation between Member States in the prevention, preparedness and response to accidents.

Accidental Marine Pollution

As a consequence of the serious incidents involving marine pollution that have occurred, the Member States have since many years been cooperating in this area and have established ability to respond to the incidents. However, no Member State has resources enough to deal with a major oil spill on its own. Mutual use of available resources is therefore a necessity.

In support of the Member States the Community has developed an Action Plan and the Commission is playing a role of significant importance in this area. One instrument is the Community Task Force which can provide assistance utilising experts drawn from the different Member States. A proposal for a Framework for Dealing with Accidental Marine Pollution is being prepared to enable systematic and consolidated action.

The Delta Plan, Netherlands.
Source : Benelux Press.

Natural Disasters

The risks and threats posed by natural disasters have a tendency to increase. The combination of this and the vulnerability of modern society calls for a more extensive use of risk assessment as well as improved preventive and preparedness measures. The community takes an active role in promoting development and facilitating assistance in case of natural disasters.

However, each Member State is responsible for such actions, including the implementation of land-use planning and development mechanisms, required for the reduction of effects from natural disasters. In 1953, for instance, Northern Europe suffered violent coastal flooding which cost many lives. The States affected later introduced a system of coastal defences and preventative features like the Delta Plan and the Thames Barrage. Projects like this require a cross-border approach.

- each Member State is responsible for the conduct of civil protection within its own territory
- risk assessment is an instrument for prevention and preparedness measures
- cooperation is well established for dealing with cases of accidental marine pollution
- for the reduction of the effects of natural disasters mechanisms such as landuse planning are used

Facts and Trends
Living earth

oil is far more than an inanimate base on which human beings can develop their economic activities. It is a complete ecosystem in itself. The inhabitants of this dark world range from bacteria to fungus and from worms to small mammals.

Making soil is a long-term proposition. It takes between 1,000 and 10,000 years to create just 30 cm of earth. To all intents and purposes, therefore, soil is very much a non-renewable resource.

Pollution and contamination

It is only recently that we have begun to appreciate the importance of soil. Because it is static, it is the ideal receptacle for a great many pollutants, which build up in the earth until it is saturated. Soil acts as a staging post in the secret life of certain heavy metals, sustaining their toxic impact on every link of the food chain.

Soil pollution has a variety of causes, from acid deposits and excessive use of fertilisers and pesticides to the storage and dumping of materials on industrial sites, the disposal of domestic and industrial waste and nuclear contamination. The vulnerability of soils also depends on their specific character. Some function better than others as buffers or filters between the surface and the groundwater layer.

Can we afford to clean up?

The cost of dealing with sites requiring urgent decontamination was estimated in 1988 at ECU 27 billion over a 15-year period. This translates into ECU 5 per citizen per year. With a price-tag like that, it is time we started thinking very seriously about prevention. Hence the need for a careful balance between exploitation and protection of the soil.

Erosion

Soil erosion is a natural phenomenon caused by water and air and is especially prevalent in the Mediterranean region. It can, however, be accelerated by deforestation and inappropriate agricultural practices. The cost of erosion, including the loss of water resources, reduced agricultural output and flood damage, has been estimated at ECU 280 million a year. The cost of restoring plant cover and the fertility of the soil has been calculated at around ECU 3 billion over a period of 15-20 years.

Erosion and pollution are the main problems affecting soil quality in Europe. The quality of soil as a natural resource has deteriorated alarmingly more or less throughout the EU.

- - - - - - - - -

Soil is an ecosystem.
Some 18 to 40 tons of earth a year are digested by 4 tons of worms per hectare of soil. Subterranean flora and fauna transform organic matter into humus and mix it with minerals. They also aerate the soil, which benefits plant life.
Source : Dobris.

SOIL

Europe in action

Which soil?

'Soil protection' refers to a wide variety of soil types, irrespective of the specific use to which they are put. Soil is a complex and dynamic system, the vulnerability of which depends on its specific character (sandy, moist, acid, clayey, silty, etc.) and its ability to store up or filter pollutants. Rather than talking about 'protecting' these dynamic, complex and heterogeneous ecosystems, it is better to focus on their specific use (agriculture, forestry, industry) and the problems that arise from this use.

Acidification

The main cause of soil acidification is atmospheric and comes from the burning of fossil fuels and industrial emissions. Its impact on soil is not visible to the naked eye. In forests, for instance, the tops of trees (the canopy) acts as a filter, concentrating toxic products like aluminium.

The main threat acidification poses to soil is the contamination of surface and groundwater, which has serious implications for aquatic life and for our drinking water reserves. In the long run, some soils gradually lose their buffering capacity, accelerating the passage of heavy metals into the groundwater. Acidification also reduces the fertility of soil but this can be offset using fertilisers. The filtration capacity of the soil, by contrast, cannot be restored.

The European Community has worked hard to reduce toxic emissions, whether industrial in origin or caused by the burning of fuel. The Commission adopted a draft framework directive in 1993 designed to prevent pollution from large industrial plants and to reduce their general environmental impact. The strategy to be pursued involves adapting industrial plants to reduce emission levels. As far as fuels are concerned, the Community has already introduced legislation to reduce emissions from diesel motors. Other directives meanwhile, target the sulphur and lead emitted by vehicle engines and by industry and waste incinerators.

Agriculture

Certain farming methods can cause a significant number of environmental problems - especially those affecting soil. Erosion, which effects the entire planet, can be increased by ploughing parallel to slopes, neglecting hedgerows or terrace cultivation, increasing field sizes, using machines that are too heavy and compact the soil and the late sowing of winter cereals. Increased erosion can only be combated by adopting appropriate farming practices.

Modern agriculture has had to become more intensive to meet the demands of a steadily growing population. Pesticides and nitrogenous fertilisers cannot be used, however, without some risk to soil, groundwater and even the cultivation they are supposed to promote.

The 'Nitrates Directive' in 1991, introduced an agricultural code of practice with the aim of reducing nitrate use. The practice of spreading purification sludge on fields is covered by a directive, which regulates the level of heavy metals permitted in the soil. Finally, although pesticide use as such is not yet controlled at European level, it is still affected by a directive, which established permissible pesticide levels in drinking water.

Industrial pollution

Industrial activity, present or past, often results in localised soil pollution. The most frequently encountered pollutants include metals, chemicals, oil and tar, pesticides, explosive gases, radioactive materials, active biological matter and asbestos. They are produced by industry and by dumping - legal or otherwise.

In the mid-1980s, the European Community began to draw up a list of contaminated sites. Around 25% of the 200,000 hectares identified had been used for metal or coal production. The cost of restoring these sites has been calculated at over ECU 100 billion. What's more, the situation in Eastern Europe is likely to be every bit as bad, if not worse. We urgently have to find a balance between affordable decontamination and addressing the health risks posed by the current situation.

Radioactive contamination

Throughout the world, all soils contain radioactive substances. The typical average concentrations of potassium 40 is about 300 bequerel per kilogram, the average concentrations of uranium 238 and thorium 232 are about 40 bequerel per kilogram for each radionuclide.

Radionuclides in the soil can lead to the exposure of man to ionising radiation via direct irradiation from the ground and radionuclides accumulated in some food chains. This became of concern in the fif-

ties and the sixties, as a consequence of the deposition by athmospheric test of atomic weapons. Most of such tests took place between 1948 and 1963.

The 1957 Treaty establishing the European Atomic Energy Community, the Euratom Treaty, requires, in its Article 35, Member States to establish the facilities necessary to carry out continuous monitoring of the levels of radioactivity in the air, water and soil, and to ensure compliance with the European Community Basic Safety Standards.

The explosion of the Chernobyl reactor on 26 April 1986 and the subsequent fire, which lasted for about two weeks, caused severe contamination of three large territories, mainly what are now the three independant republics of Belarus, Russia and Ukrain.

As a consequence of the accident, many people were evacuated and hectares of agricultural, natural and semi-natural

Former open fields, Slagelse, Sjælland, eastern Denmark. Source : redrawn from J. Meeus.

Organic matter is vital to the balance of the soil. It retains water, acts as a nutrient reserve and forms a chemical buffer. Intensive cultivation can reduce organic matter and diminish overall biological activity and diversity. One way of addressing these problems is to incorporate fallow periods in the rotation plan and to replace stubble burning with burial. Europe's policy of encouraging fallow periods can only benefit farmland.

----

land were completely restricted from use. Cooperative programmes involving institutions and scientists from the European Union and from the most affected republics were set up to study the behaviour and the transfer of radionuclides in the contaminated environment. Management systems were developed for mitigating the effect of the contamination.

Siberian tundra.
Source : J. S. Grove, WWF.

SOIL

Taking responsibility

Member states

Up to now, soil protection policies have concentrated on maintaining fertility (essentially for the benefit of agriculture and forestry), protecting water reserves and preventing the damage inflicted by human economic activity (industry and waste disposal).

Some countries (Austria, Italy, the Netherlands and Switzerland) already have laws which place the emphasis on soil as such and on the causes of soil degradation, such as overgrazing. The oldest laws of this kind are undoubtedly those designed to reduce soil erosion (Iceland, 1895). In more recent years, legislation has been produced to control soil pollution. The Netherlands and Denmark, meanwhile, have passed laws requiring the clean-up of polluted sites.

Even so, it is still unusual for other forms of soil degradation to be taken into account. Legislators face the difficulty that, unlike air or water, soil actually belongs to someone. As environmental law stands at present, soil protection has to be negotiated between the responsible authorities and the owners or occupants.

International co-operation

Analysis of soil degradation and pollution reveals the need for national and international action to protect it. Some problems extend across frontiers and can only be dealt with if all the countries involved work together. This is particularly the case with toxic substances of atmospheric origin. Several programmes in this field have been initiated in Europe, involving the OECD, the Council of Europe, UNEP, and other organisations.

Soil quality could continue to deteriorate in the future, in spite of the programmes initiated by member states. Environmental policies and soil protection measures still have only limited objectives and we lack the information we need to form a complete picture of the current situation. The absence of Community policy in this particular field is due to the principle of subsidiarity.

Outlook

Soil protection policy in the future will have to take fuller account of the 'multifunctionality' principle. This is already the case in the Netherlands, Germany and Switzerland, where soil is not only considered in terms of how it can be exploited. After all, soils are not just distinguished by their use, but also by the specific way in which they respond to the different problems. Taking account of the vulnerability of the soil when planning land use would minimise the impact of human activities.

Experts agree that the first thing we need to do is to gain a better understanding of the problem and its causes and effects. We don't even have a complete list of contaminated sites in Europe. Once the problems have been established and the trends identified, we will be able to set up monitoring networks for vulnerable soils and to develop effective protection methods. For the time being, finally, we have to protect soil from permanent damage and only to use it for purposes that are reversible. The precaution principle is the first step towards taking fuller account of the suitability and vulnerability of soil.

Cork oaks (quercus suber) in Portugal.
Source : D. Wascher.

Facts and Trends
Our fragile and threatened heritage

Europe may be the second smallest continent, but from the Atlantic plains to the Russian Steppes and from Lapland to the Mediterranean, it is home to an immense variety of ecosystems, both natural and semi-natural. These include increasingly rare examples of forests, peat bogs and marshlands that have so far been untouched by human activity. Others, such as grasslands, lakes, rivers, marine ecosystems, mountains, deserts, tundra, dunes and cliffs form a palette of landscapes and environments that nurture an abundance of plant and animal varieties, some of which aren't found anywhere else.

This natural wealth is not distributed evenly across Europe. There are fewer species in Northern Europe, for instance, which was covered in ice until 10,000 years ago. The Mediterranean basin, by contrast, is teeming with plants, many of them specific to that region. The small French Département of Alpes Maritimes alone boasts more species of flowering plant (2,500) than the whole of the United Kingdom, which is 100 times its size.

Humans have been reshaping the countryside for thousands of years, clearing forests, cultivating the soil, draining marshes, altering the course of rivers, excavating mines, laying roads and building towns. Our environment is becoming increasingly artificial. Many animals and plants have had to seek refuge in areas that are not attractive to humans. But even these natural enclaves are under increasing threat. Rare habitats are deteriorating, while others have totally disappeared under growing pressure from human activities. As people have altered their environment, they have increasingly jeopardised the fragile balance of nature on which we depend - the composition of the air we breathe, the CO_2 which is processed by plants, the purity of our water, which filters through the soil, and the entire balance of a food chain in which we are merely the final link. We share the natural stage with other species and habitats. As we approach the end of the 20th century, the review of our performance, whether in terms of habitats or species, is scathing. Habitats are fragmenting and becoming rarer. They are less and less able to harbour wildlife. And as small populations become increasingly isolated, they can no longer maintain the links they need to ensure vital genetic exchange. The number of plant and animal species threatened with extinction is growing all the time.

Species facing extinction

Animals and plants interact closely with the environments on which they depend. Species have always appeared and disappeared naturally or following catastrophic events such as volcanic eruptions or an encroaching ice age. For the past 10,000 years, however, the main agent of change has been humanity, which has constantly created new ecological conditions. This process was very successful, at least until the last century, when changes began to occur at too fast a pace for wildlife to adapt. The result has been an alarming reduction in the number of animal and plant species more or less throughout Europe. In the case of localised species, disappearance from a given region is synonymous with extinction.

The brown bear of the French Pyrenees, for instance, only a few of which remain, looks doomed to disappear, despite a recent, limited attempt at reintroduction.

We don't inherit the earth, but we do need to preserve it for our children. For that reason, we urgently need to protect our fragile and threatened heritage. Nature knows nothing of walls or frontiers and so it has to be protected on a global and supranational basis. Europe's actions are based entirely on recognition of this fact.

- Forest currently accounts for around 33% of total land area;
- Marshland and peat bogs have disappeared in many Southern and Western European countries - Spain has lost 60%;
- Between a third and half of all European fish, reptiles, mammals and amphibians are under threat;
- The total area of protected sites in Europe has tripled since 1972. Many of these are small or fragmented, however, and are not effectively protected for want of money or personnel.

Brown bear (Ursus arctos). Source : P. Heineman, WWF.

Europe in action
Nature and Europe go back a long way

Several trends can be identified in the development of European nature conservation policies in recent years. There has been a movement:

- From the protection of species towards the protection of habitats;
- From the protection of species and habitats towards the protection of the natural processes on which they depend;
- From nature protection as a self-contained exercise towards the integration of nature conservation as a standard feature of environmental planning and management in every sector of the economy;
- From local or national programmes towards co-ordinated programmes of international co-operation, and
- From the conservation of nature for its aesthetic and scientific value towards a recognition of the eco-systems, species and biodiversity that are required for sustainable development.

Species and habitats

Since 1979, the Birds Directive has imposed a duty on Member States to protect the habitats of their wild bird populations. All wild bird species are protected under this directive. Hunting is allowed for certain species but only under controlled conditions. There is a particular obligation to designate special protection areas for 181 rare and vulnerable species as well as for migratory birds (nearly 1700 sites covering 110 000 Km2 to date). Experts, however, agree that an area twice as large would be needed to create a network capable of sustaining migratory species.

The **Habitats Directive**, adopted in 1992, the year of

Peregrine falcon. Source : W. Moeller, WWF.

The peregrine falcon perches at the top of the food chain, where it has suffered from the accumulation of toxic residues in its prey resulting from the large-scale use of insecticides since the 1950s. A ban on organochlorines (which damages egg-shells) has helped the population of this predator to begin growing again. But other threats like poachers and collectors still hang over the heads of these regal creatures.

the Rio summit on the environment and development, is the main Community instrument safeguarding biodiversity. It broadens the scope for nature protection to other species and includes the conservation of habitats as an objective in its own right for the first time. The major challenge of this directive is the creation of the European ecological network of natural areas, called "Natura 2000". All areas designated under the Birds Directive also form part of the Natura 2000 network.

Natura 2000, the European Ecological Network

Each Member State is responsible for identifying and designating as Special Areas of Conservation sites which are important for the protection of the species and habitats covered by the Directive. These areas will benefit from statutory or contractual measures and, where appropriate, management plans which will ensure

their long-term preservation by integrating human activities into a sustainable development strategy.

Each Member State can choose the mechanisms it uses to participate in this joint enterprise. The Commission is helping to set up the network and ensure that the common goals become reality.

Nature and agriculture go hand in hand

The fragmentation and shrinkage of habitats is having the effect of isolating populations from one another. This phenomenon is known as 'insularisation' and results in genetic impoverishment and ultimately the extinction of populations as they are forced to breed amongst themselves. The solution is to enable habitats to communicate with one another by means of wider countryside measures. This allows threatened species to circulate and to escape the trap of insularisation.

Europe must also take full account of nature conservation nowadays in its economic development schemes. It is acknowledged, for instance, that certain EU measures, particularly agricultural policy, have had a direct and sometimes harmful impact on wildlife. From now on, European projects should respect those habitats and species designated as important by the Birds and Habitats Directives.

International actions

The European Community plays an active part in the drafting and implementation of international conventions on the environment. International actions of this kind take the form of treaties or programmes embracing the whole world or focusing on specific regions.

The initiatives in which Europe is involved notably includes the CITES Convention on trade in endangered species, the Berne Convention, which aims to protect wildlife and natural habitats and the Bonn Convention on migratory species and, more recently, the Rio Convention on biodiversity which inspired the EU biodiversity strategy.

Finally, by enshrining the importance of nature in its legislation, Europe is displaying a new recognition of the value of our natural heritage. Thereby, the Community is demonstrating to its neighbours a real commitment to efficient nature conservation.

Biogeographic Regions
(Council Directive 92/43/EEC)

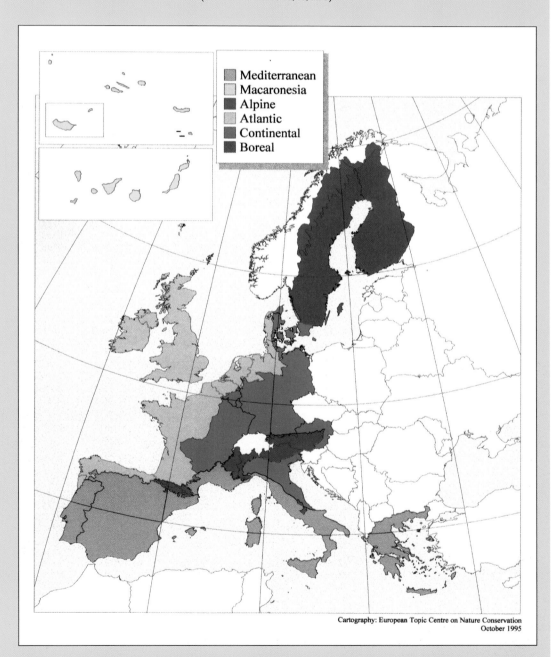

Legend:
- Mediterranean
- Macaronesia
- Alpine
- Atlantic
- Continental
- Boreal

Cartography: European Topic Centre on Nature Conservation
October 1995

Taking responsibility

National action

Member States and regions did not wait for Europe to act. They began by granting protected status to species threatened by farming methods, hunters and collectors, before extending this protection to sites viewed as exemplary habitats. These nature reserves vary widely in terms of both size and the degree of protection they offer.

Member States should translate European Directives into their own national law. The Birds and Habitats Directives have placed a duty on them to develop new protection measures.

Habitats are also being protected by incorporating important sites in networks and by taking full account of nature when drafting policies in other sectors like agriculture, transport and energy. Member States and local authorities can do a great deal to protect and promote their natural heritage by enshrining it in their economic strategy and at all levels of town and country planning. The aim of European Union policy is to ensure that nature protection is given its rightful place amongst the priorities of every political decision-maker, from the drafting of regional economic development plans to the issuing of a simple building permit.

Europe

European policy on nature conservation has to contend with both a plethora of local initiatives (nature reserves, protected species, etc.) and a critical lack of data. Strategies, regulations and actions to protect nature in the future will lack direction unless we have comparable information concerning the state of ecosystems, species and the results of protective measures that have already been taken locally. The creation of a European Environment Agency based in Copenhagen ought to provide the European Community with an effective tool in this field.

Citizens

Wildlife organisations have done a great deal of remarkable work over the years, gathering information on species, maintaining reserves and raising public and government awareness of environmental problems. We would know considerably less about nature without these enthusiastic ornithologists, botanists and naturalists who have been contributing to our scientific knowledge for generations. Individual citizens might worry that on their own they can contribute little more than a love and understanding of nature, and that decision-making is something that goes on above their heads. Surely they can do little more than recycle their refuse and buy environmentally friendly products? In reality, you don't have to be an expert to promote nature. Anyone can do so by creating a natural garden, a pond or a little pocket of greenery which - even in the middle of the city - can act as a way-station for birds and butterflies or as a home for some native plant. In this way, citizens can provide natural oases that will contribute to nature protection everywhere in the Community.

Management of marshlands (Episy, France). Source : Ecosphère (France).

Facts and Trends
Planet Earth - the new Ark

Biodiversity has been a fashionable idea ever since the spotlight fell on it during the Rio Earth Summit in June 1992. As with all fashions, however, there is a danger that people will eventually get bored with it. To make matters worse, 'biodiversity' is frequently mixed up with 'nature' or 'environment'. In reality, it is much more complex than that.

Biodiversity basically refers to all the different varieties and forms of life. It breaks down into three levels - diversity of ecosystems, species and genes. In Europe alone, there are an estimated 2,500 types of habitat or ecosystems and 215,000 species, 90% of which are invertebrates. As for genetic diversity, the numbers involved are quite simply staggering, especially if we take account of all the potential gene combinations.

If biodiversity simply meant 'all forms of life', however, it would be synonymous with 'biosphere'. There's more to it than that. Biodiversity is a property of the living world - a genetic reservoir that enables it to evolve and adapt constantly. In short, it is the net result of three billion years of evolution.

Life itself is running out steam

People are becoming aware nowadays of the impact their activities have on their surroundings, particularly the living world. The rise of agriculture led to the creation and management of new environments and actually added to biodiversity. Humans created clearings, grazing land and hedgerows, all of them opportunities that have been gratefully exploited by countless plant and animal species.

And so it remained until very recently. In our own time, however, changes in agricultural practice (monoculture, fertilisers, pesticides and so forth) have joined a whole series of other human environmental pressures, from the pollution of the air, water and soil, to urbanisation and mass tourism. The economic imperatives of our society care little for the value and role of biodiversity.

Urgent need

Since Rio '92, everyone has agreed that we are suffering a global loss of biodiversity and that we urgently need to slow down this process. The reasons for acting are, however, both numerous and diverse, reflecting the complexity of the subject. In one sense, biodiversity is a resource (in terms of agriculture, animal husbandry and pharmaceuticals) that has to be preser-

Cactus and aloes in Almeria, Spain. Source : Spectrum Colour Library.

ved if we are to have a useful stock capable of meeting our future needs. Biodiversity is also relevant to the field of genetic manipulation. This is an area with an immense future, but whether this will prove positive or negative depends very much on what we choose to do with it.

As far as 'natural' biodiversity is concerned, solving the problem will also require measures to protect ecosystems and species and the setting up of a network of sites to promote genetic exchange. Most institutions and states have already acknowledged the vital need to incorporate these ideas in the sectors implicated in biodiversity loss, such as agriculture, transport and energy. In fact, the problem touches every field of human activity. The complexity of the solutions matches that of the problem, but the first step we have to make is an intellectual one. Before we can do anything else, we have to learn to view the earth's living riches not only as a resource for humanity, but above all as a unique heritage to be protected.

Distribution of higher plants by continent. Source : IUCN.

CONTINENT/REGION	PLANT NUMBER
Latin America (Mexico through S America)	85.000
Tropical & subtropical Africa	45.000
Tropical & subtropical Asia	50.000
Australia	15.000
North America	17.000
Europe	12.500

BIODIVERSITY

Europe in action

Abundant life

Despite its relatively small surface area and the fact that part of its territory was completely covered in ice barely ten thousand years ago, Europe presents naturalists with a huge variety of landscapes, ecosystems and species, many of which are endemic (not found elsewhere). The level of biodiversity in the North is not so high because of its relatively recent glaciation, and so the main nuclei are located in the Mediterranean basin and the territories leading to the foothills of the Caucasus. Europe boasts roughly 5,000 endemic varieties of plant, although many of these exist in more than one member state. Consequently, protecting them entails cross-border co-operation. At the same time, a great many domesticated plants and the genetic material they contain come from countries other than those where they are cultivated today. All the more reason for formulating an international policy in this field.

Legislating on a brand new concept

The European Community approved the Convention on Biological Diversity signed in Rio in June 1992. The aims of the convention are to preserve biological diversity, to engage in the sustainable use of its elements and to ensure the fair distribution of the benefits arising from the exploitation of genetic resources. Although these objectives may seem clear enough, the way in which they are to be achieved is far from established. Unless a specific common programme is adopted to this end, the implementation of the Rio Convention will depend largely on the Bird and Habitats Directives and on other EC measures to protect nature.

Genetic manipulation

In this entirely new field, whose commercial, medical and environmental implications remain difficult to predict, the Community has chosen to legislate in such a way as to protect the health of its citizens and the environment, but also to create a single unified market for biotechnology.

The fragile balance of biodiversity

'The different species that make up an ecosystem may be compared with the countless rivets, all apparently the same, that give an aeroplane its strength. If we were to spring those rivets, one by one, there would not be an immediate catastrophe. Sooner or later, however, disaster would inevitably strike.' Erlich & Erlich, 1981.

Agriculture and biodiversity

Incorporating biodiversity in other European policies will also become a priority, particularly with respect to the Common Agricultural Policy. This

has already been the case as far as nature conservation is concerned since the reform of the CAP in 1992 (2078/92). The measures arising from this have led primarily to a reduction in the amount of land under cultivation. More recently, Member States have undertaken to promote 'green' agricultural practices. Local programmes have emerged to encourage less 'aggressive' and environmentally harmful farming. These new programmes are long-term in character. They aim to reduce the level of soil enrichment and to manage the environment in a way that conserves nature. Measures of this kind were successfully introduced in 1994 and even before in certain countries (UK, Germany, Netherlands).

One way to promote biodiversity in agriculture is to support the production of the kind of old or local varieties that have gradually been disappearing from the market, where they have been replaced by standard products.

Forestry and biodiversity

Financial support is offered for the reforestation and management of neglected woodland

Wetlands in Iceland. Source : Mercay, WWF.

areas. Commercial forestry is encouraged, of course, but the planting of several different varieties is encouraged, as is sustainable management, to avoid the negative side-effects of monoculture.

Action on all fronts

The battle for biodiversity has to be fought in the many different sectors that threaten it. Habitats and species suffer from air, water and soil pollution and from the intensity of many economic activities. If we are to shield a greater area from human activities (barely 2,000,000 km² are currently protected) and to reduce the damage inflicted on all levels of life, we have to act in all sectors (agriculture, forestry, transport, energy, tourism and finance) and to address the problems of regional development, soil erosion, desertification, air and water pollution. The complexity of the task facing us is clear, as is the need for a 'multidisciplinary' approach to solving it.

The enemies of biodiversity

Many human activities inflict irreversible damage on key habitats for certain insects, small mammals and wild plants which are deemed unprofitable and hence undesirable. Biodiversity is damaged by:
- The canalisation of rivers and the destruction of river banks.
- Intensive agriculture and the use of pesticides.
- The increasing uniformity of the agricultural landscape (disappearance of hedgerows and copses).
- The draining of marches and wetlands.
Alternative practices have now been proposed to farmers and foresters in the hope of reconciling economic development with the need to promote biodiversity.

The example of the Loire 'Europe's last untamed river' Haute-Loire, France

The Loire rises in the Massif Central and flows a thousand kilometres to the sea. In the process, it drains 20% of all French waters. Many birds, plants and invertebrates, some of which are rare or vulnerable, have found a refuge in its alluvial plain, formed by canals, oxbow lakes, islands and sandbanks. Salmon, which are a migratory species, have suffered badly from pollution and the construction of barrages. Nowadays, only one tributary

(the Allier) remains accessible to salmon, whose population has dropped to a mere 10% of what it once was. In addition to barrages built to protect the surrounding land against flooding, the Loire's ecosystem has also had to contend with sand extraction and the impact of intensive agriculture on its plain.

The Loire is now protected by several programmes including the Berne Convention and the Ramsar Convention, which led to the cancellation of two barrage projects. Thanks to the European Union's LIFE programme, eight conservation projects have been set up along the Loire and the Allier. The aim of these projects is to conserve the river's biological wealth and the quality of its water. At the same time, we still need to raise people's awareness to allow sustainable use of the river and its resources. Reconciling development with nature conservation is another way of promoting biodiversity.

Source : M. Rautkari, WWF.

Taking responsibility

Countries

Each country that has signed the Rio Convention has undertaken to develop strategies and action plans. As far as the law is concerned, this means regulating access to genetic resources, intellectual property rights and technology transfers. From the economic point of view, it is useful to consider biodiversity in terms of the economic utility of its preservation. A shift in viewpoint of this kind would highlight the importance of biodiversity as a resource and lend it additional weight as an economic asset. From the classic viewpoint of nature protection, conservation measures ought to reflect the need to act at the core of each sector (energy, agriculture, transport and planning). The application of green farming practices is very much a step in the right direction. These reduce inputs and lessen the burden on our aquifers and protect environments like hedgerows, copses and peat-bogs that encourage wildlife. However, after years of an agricultural policy that was geared towards self-sufficiency in food , it won't be easy to change attitudes.

Europe

Europe hasn't yet launched any specific initiatives to put the Rio convention into practice. Many of its environmental campaigns do, however, help to promote biodiversity. The two main instruments at the EU's disposal are the Bird and Habitats Directives, which have proved immensely effective from the conservation point of view. Europe is well aware that it needs to shift its emphasis in the near future towards harmonising data gathered in each member state. Our understanding of biodiversity is even more vague than that of 'nature' in general.

Scientists and citizens

Geneticists enjoy the almost divine power of manipulating living matter. They must be fully aware of the implications and must also comply with a rigorous set of ethics, despite the commercial or political pressures that might be exerted on them. Take the moratorium, for instance, that the scientific community placed on the manipulation of human genes a few years ago. Although biodiversity is a highly specialised concept, which scientists would not like to see debased, its basic principles have already reached a wide audience. In fact, this is a field in which all of us can act at our own level. We can manage our own micro-territory, for instance, planting indigenous varieties, gardening extensively rather than intensively or rejecting aggressive fertilisers. The choices we make as consumers are also important. We can opt for local, organic or non-standardised products and for rustic or old varieties. In short, there are countless ways in which the ordinary citizen can help protect biodiversity through his or her everyday actions.

Lowland Wetland Poitevin Marshes, France.
Source : Michael St Maur, Sheil.

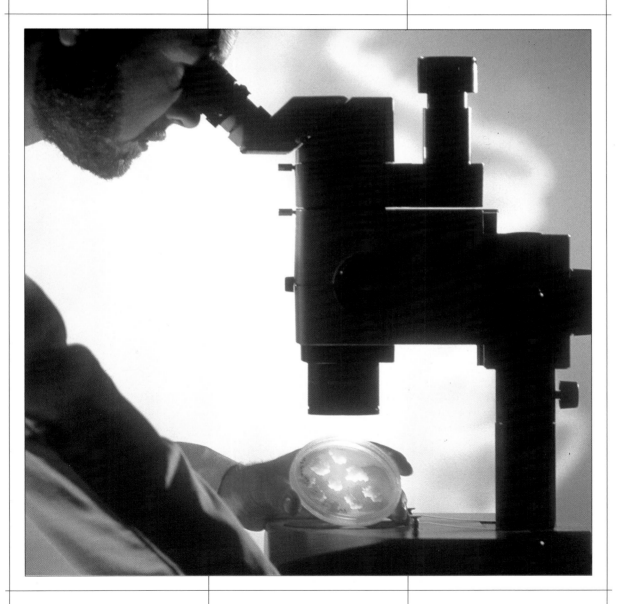

Facts and Trends
Chemical and genetic time-bomb?

Chemicals - we can't do without them !
Our laboratories currently turn out no fewer than 13 million synthetic compounds. Some mimic natural substances while others are entirely artificial. Chemicals are used in every sector of the economy, from agriculture and food to textiles, paper and pharmaceuticals. Around 100,000 chemical products are available on the European market and the industry launches two to three hundred more every year.

Chemicals produced in the EU and EFTA countries (by volume). Source : CEFIC, 1991.

GROUP OF CHEMICALS	PER CENT
Basic organics	19,7
Pharmaceuticals	19,7
Plastics	11,0
Inorganics	7,2
Perfumes and cosmetics	6,4
Paints	4,7
Detergents	3,7
Fibres	3,7
Dyes	1,6
Others	22,3

The complexity of chemical products and the pace of their development have not been matched in recent years by systematic research into their environmental impact. Serious and undesirable effects have, however, been detected in both human health and the environment. Toxic products have been found in the air, water and soil, not to mention the food we eat. Between 1977 and 1987, accidents involving chemicals resulted in 5,000 recorded deaths, 100,000 injuries and the evacuation of 620,000 people.

Care and foresight

Fortunately, relatively few chemicals have such dire potential. If they are used in a controlled and responsible way, the vast majority of citizens have nothing to fear. Nevertheless, more and more care is needed if we are to avoid horrific accidents such as those that occurred at Bhopal, India in 1984 and Seveso, Italy in 1976. If disasters are to be prevented, there is an urgent need for accurate scientific modelling of the potential long-term impact of chemicals on health and the environment.

Genetic modification

The latest gene technology means we can now transfer inherited characteristics from one organism to another. This produces Genetically Modified Organisms (GMOs) - bacteria, fungi, viruses, plants, insects, fish or mammals, whose genetic material has been artificially altered in order to increase resistance, yield or some other physical property.

Once a GMO has been released into nature (or brought onto the market), it might prove more successful in evolutionary terms than its natural counterparts. The repercussions of such competition are both unpredictable and irreversible.

Doomsday scenarios apart, it is plain that the benefits genetic engineering can bring to humankind must be properly managed if health and the environment are to be protected.

Source : Benelux Press

Hazard warning!

Chemicals can be inflammable, explosive or corrosive. They threaten us with allergies, poisoning, cancer and genetic mutation. Some damage our reproductive, nervous and immune systems. And chemicals can attack individuals, whole populations and even future generations.

Europe in action

Prevention better than cure

Europe's concern for this issue is evident from the speed with which it built up a formidable legislative arsenal to deal with hazardous substances. Some observers view dangerous chemicals as the gravest environmental threat of all.

Classification, labelling and packaging of hazardous substances

A framework directive was adopted in 1992 which covers all substances and preparations defined as explosive, oxidising, inflammable, toxic, corrosive, irritating, sensitising, carcinogenic, mutagenic, harmful to reproduction or environmentally damaging. The directive also set the new objective of evaluating the risks that chemicals pose to human beings and the environment. Manufacturers and distributors are now obliged to provide the authorities with detailed technical information, to state any undesirable effects, and to draw up safety instructions and packaging and labelling information.

At the same time, the directive introduced stricter standards for the packaging and labelling of hazardous substances. Packaging must be sufficiently robust to prevent leakage or corrosion during handling, while labels have to include the name of the substance, one or more warning symbols, details of potential hazards and safety recommendations.

It established new principles for evaluating the risks to which hazardous chemicals expose human beings and the environment.

Use and marketing

The use of hazardous substances is governed by a 1976 framework directive designed to protect the public and the environment from certain hazardous chemicals. The appendix listed a number of products which could no longer be sold directly to the public and whose use was now strictly limited. Supplementary directives have restricted the use of products like asbestos, mercury, cadmium and benzene (in toys) and have imposed labelling and packaging requirements (particularly for detergents, insecticides and perfumes).

Lab technician preparing cultures.
Source : Science Photo Library

Tackling genetics

There is basically no limit to the potential of genetic engineering. In theory, a gene from any species can be implanted in any other. Genetic manipulation is already used in agriculture and the food industry, in pharmaceuticals and decontaminants and in the production of new materials and energy sources.

Europe has taken a precautionary approach, introducing legislation designed to protect its citizens' health and the environment while simultaneously creating a unified market for biotechnology. A directive on the contained use of genetically modified micro-organisms covers all activities relating to GMO's, at both research and industrial level. A directive on the deliberate release into the environment of genetically modified organisms requires environmental evaluation and step-by-step approval for the dissemination of GMO's. The directive covers all such releases, whether small or large in scale, commercial or otherwise. Its main aim is risk management. As with all other technologies, the risks associated with genetic engineering have to be identified, evaluated and appropriate measures taken. The directive's approach to risk management is based on the step-by-step development and testing of new organisms, the risk and impact of which have to be analysed case by case.

Detailed and strict labelling for all hazardous substances. Source : Benelux Press

Import and export

Regulations adopted by the Community in 1992 have created a joint information system on imports and exports of certain chemicals that are banned or severely restricted because of their potentially harmful impact on human health and the environment. When a product is to be transported to a new destination for the first time, Member States are now obliged to inform the importing country of any potential hazards no later than 30 days before the date of export. The regulations also oblige exporters of hazardous chemicals to package and label products destined for export in the same way as those sold on the Community market.

Plant protection products

A directive on the placing of plant protection products on the market was adopted in July 1991 and created a harmonised system for approving products in this field. Basically speaking, the directive prevents plant protection products from being sold unless they meet certain specified 'quality' criteria, according to which they must not have an unacceptable impact on human beings, animals or the environment.

Genetics : what for ?

The most common of the 16 varieties of genetically modified plants cultivated in Europe are turnips, maize, potatoes and sugar beet. The added genes often relate to herbicide resistance (50%), while in other cases they are concerned with the sterility of male plants.

Taking responsibility

Hazardous substances: an international concern

In 1984, the NRC (National Research Council) in the United States published statistics on the toxicity of around 50,000 chemicals currently in use in that country. Another study (USEPA, 1991) highlighted the fact that the majority of substances discharged into water are industrial and chemical in origin (60%). The NRC figures also show how little information is available on the toxicity of chemical substances. What information there is tends to be limited to pesticides, cosmetics, medicines and food additives.

We can't draw up a systematic and detailed review of the risks associated with chemical products without first collating all the available information on existing substances. This is an immense task and so international programmes have been set up to gather data and co-ordinate results. Programmes of this kind are our primary source of information on hazardous substances.

A special legal register has been set up to record data from 12 countries and six international organisations. In 1989, it contained 42,000 records on over 8,000 substances.

Biotechnology and the Earth Summit

The problem of access to genetic resources was raised in the text of the Rio Biodiversity Convention which sets out to regulate access to these resources, to protect intellectual property rights on living materials and to promote technology transfers.

Biotechnology, Europe and its member states

The Rio Biodiversity Convention recognises *the sovereign rights of States over their natural resources* but obliges them to *create conditions to facilitate access to genetic resources for environmentally sound uses by other parties.*

As far as Europe is concerned, member states must notify the Community of the release of genetically modified organisms. This duty represents a unique opportunity for tracking deliberate GMO releases from the very beginning. In other words, Europe has been quick to equip itself with a powerful instrument for controlling the risks associated with genetic engineering - a prerequisite for the environmental management of all biotechnology.

Source : Benelux Press

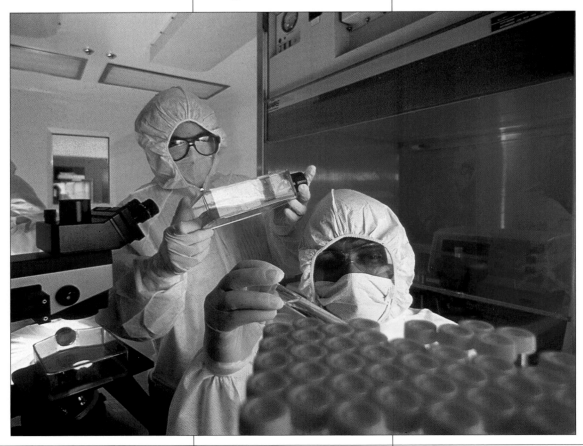

Facts and Trends
Health and environment

"**H**ealth is a state of physical, mental and social well-being and not simply the absence of illness or infirmity."** (World Health Organisation (WHO) Huge advances in public health were made in the 19th and early 20th century thanks to improved sanitation, working conditions and hygiene. In some cases, the introduction of a few hygiene measures had a spectacular impact on outbreaks of disease and other previously intractable health problems.

An inseparable trio : health, pollution and the environment

We have a thorough understanding nowadays of the link between health and concentrations of pathogenic substances. The relationship between health and everyday pollution levels is, by contrast, a good deal more complex. Many diseases are caused by a combination of several factors - economic, social and lifestyle (nutrition, smoking, etc.) - making it difficult to isolate the specific environmental elements.

We can, however, draw up a long list of hazards known to contribute to an unhealthy environment, including food-poisoning, occupational diseases, allergies, smoking, cardiovascular disease caused by an unhealthy lifestyle and cancers induced by radiation or asbestos. The European Community and the World Health Organisation (WHO) have focused particular attention on air pollution, water contamination and road accidents. 'Environmental' factors like this are responsible for a steadily growing number of public health problems.

Air pollution

A large proportion of Europe's population is affected by polluted air, particularly in urban areas. The number of respiratory problems (such as asthma and bronchitis) rises sharply when particular exposure levels are exceeded. This can lead to hospitalisation and even death.

Water pollution

Polluted water, such as polluted bathing water or insufficient quality of drinking water from the tap, may affect human health in various ways. Whereas these two issues are specifically tackled by the Bathing Water and the Drinking Water Directives, more needs to be done to protect water as a resource. This is why the proposed Framework Water Directive expands the scope of protection to all waters.

Road accidents

These result in death, injury and long-term incapacity for a large number of Europeans every year. So acute has this problem become that road accidents are now the principal cause of death amongst 15-24 year-olds. In this respect, road safety has to be seen as a public health issue. On the other hand, although accidents cannot be attributed directly to environmental factors, the problems (such as pollution) associated with transport affect both human health and the environment.

Air pollution, water contamination and road accidents have not been picked on because of their quantitative importance, but because they provide decision-makers with certain opportunities. Preventative action in these fields represents a major investment in public health.

> Every day, 342 people are killed on our roads and 6,229 injured. Road accidents deprive society of men and women in the prime of life. Others are condemned to prolonged incapacity, families suffer intensely and costs are raised for everyone.

Europe in action
To tackle the problems at source

Air pollution, water contamination and road accidents can all be tackled at source, while appropriate technical measures can address the various problems they create.

Air pollution

Air pollution is harmful to human health - a problem that is particularly acute in the countries of Eastern Europe. It has been calculated that WHO standards for one or more atmospheric pollutants are exceeded at least once a year in 70-80% of Europe's 105 cities

air pollution also increases the risk of cancer. Asbestos, benzene and soot have all been identified as cancer-inducing by the International Agency for Research in Cancer, while diesel too is said to be 'probably' carcinogenic.

Technical advances and international conventions have helped improve air quality. Even so,

Source : Michael St Maur Sheil.

with over 500,000 inhabitants. Millions of Europeans are affected, especially those living in urban areas. Some 15% of people in these areas suffer from asthma and 7% from respiratory problems. The asthma rate rises in the most polluted cities to 23% of the population.

In addition to causing acute or chronic respiratory conditions,

WHO standards are still frequently exceeded, damaging people's health in the process. Since 1972, the Community has been acting to reduce pollutant emissions from diesel motors. Several other directives have followed, designed to reduce sulphur content and lead pollution. They cover all engine types and also target industry and incinerators. Road traffic is growing at such a rate, however, that overall emissions continue to rise in absolute

Lead

Lead has a harmful impact on health more or less throughout Europe. Statistics suggest a reduction in lead exposure in Western Europe, due primarily to the lowering of the lead content in petrol. Many people in Central and Eastern Europe, by contrast, are suffering high levels of exposure, especially those who live near heavy industrial plants. Lead retards children's mental development and causes behavioural problems. Some 400,000 children in Eastern Europe are currently believed to be affected this way.

terms, despite all these measures.

Contaminated water

Consuming water contaminated by microbiological agents can lead to a range of diseases, from gastro-enteritis to hepatitis A. Despite a series of preventative measures, cases of illness caused by the drinking of contaminated water are reported every year. Meanwhile, bathing in contaminated water may cause gastro-enteritis or skin and eye irritations.

Concentrations of agricultural nitrates in groundwater often exceed the permitted rates for consumption by children.

Many other dangerous substances find their way into our water supplies, either accidentally or through dumping. Generally speaking, however, chemical discharges are effectively controlled and seem to have less of an impact on Europeans' health than microbiological contamination. This is another field in which Europe has been actively legislating for some time now. An example is the 'Nitrates Directive' which seeks to reduce the level of agricultural nitrates in groundwater and surface water by

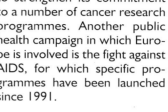
introducing an action programme and an agricultural code of good practice. Others are the 'Bathing Water Directive' and the 'Drinking Water Directive', which fixes quality standards for water destined for human consumption.

Roads kill

Road accidents are an important public health issue, even if they are not a 'disease' as such. It is impossible to ignore the specific and grave harm they inflict on people's health, especially that of young people:

- No reduction is apparent in either the frequency of accidents or their adverse impact on health;
- They are an economic burden on society, not only in terms of material damage but also of medical costs and the long-term handicaps suffered by certain victims;
- The health impact of road accidents varies from one country to another, irrespective of economic performance. That means it ought to be possible to reduce it.

Unblocking the road network

Europe is pursuing a dual policy to deal with the problems caused by transport. In the first place, it has introduced vehicle standards designed to reduce noise and toxic emissions and to improve safety. The Commission is also involved in the construction of trans-European transport networks to relieve pressure on traditional roads and is encouraging a shift in demand towards alternative forms of transport like high-speed trains and waterways.

Nutrition, cancer and AIDS.

European action in the health field is not limited to these three areas. Several directives, for instance, have been introduced to protect citizens from radioactive emissions.

Cancer is the second most important cause of death in Europe. One person in four dies of the disease and the rate is growing in most Member States. This development has prompted the European Union

to strengthen its commitment to a number of cancer research programmes. Another public health campaign in which Europe is involved is the fight against AIDS, for which specific programmes have been launched since 1991.

Europe is also active in the field of nutrition, restricting the use of certain additives, banning hormones, curtailing tobacco and alcohol advertising and regulating pharmaceutical products. Meanwhile, the EU is committed to reducing the risk of bacterial or chemical poisoning (heavy metals, pesticides, etc.).

The first European directive to address the issue of food hygiene was issued in 1964. Europe's current approach is based on the following principles:

- Preventing any contamination of fresh meat, dairy products, eggs, fish, etc.;
- Fixing the maximum permissible concentrations of certain residual chemical products;
- Inspecting the production, processing and packaging of food products in both Member States and in countries exporting to the EU.

Source : Benelux Press.

Taking responsibility

The world

Diseases don't recognise national frontiers and economic and cultural globalisation is promoting the spread of pathogens. Several international organisations are devoted to health, including the International Agency for Research in Cancer, the Red Cross and the Red Crescent. Best known, however, is probably the World Health Organisation, a UN body founded in 1948.

The WHO is known by the public for its work to combat infectious diseases like malaria, leprosy, diphtheria, tuberculosis and hepatitis in developing countries. It has a regional bureau in Copenhagen called the European Centre for Environment and Health (ECEH), which was set up in 1991. The Centre was recently commissioned to draft a report entitled 'Concern for Europe's Tomorrow' in collaboration with the European Environment Agency. The purpose was to evaluate environmental problems with health implications, to calculate the European population's exposure to these factors and to measure the extent of their impact. This joint ECEH and EEA initiative is a remarkable example of co-operation between the health and environment fields. 'Concern for Europe's Tomorrow' will provide government and NGOs with the fullest possible information on which to base their decision-making in these areas.

The ECEH's remit also includes the development of technical co-operation programmes, primarily with countries in Eastern Europe. These set out to reduce the health problems caused by environmental hazards.

Blood analysis.

Source : Benelux Press.

Europe and its Member States

When it comes to health, European institutions do not attempt to take the place of individual Member States or their respective health ministers, which support a great many public and private bodies, including institutes of hygiene and epidemiology, national child health agencies and public health laboratories. Meanwhile, a Standing Veterinary Committee, made up of representatives of each member state, advises the Commission on matters relating to its specialist field and on any emergency measures that might be required. The committee also gives permission for imports from third countries and withdraws it again whenever necessary.

The European Community does, however, oversee research and prevention programmes for cancer, AIDS (the European Centre for the Epidemiological Monitoring of AIDS is located in Paris) and drug dependency.

Facts and Trends

To be taken in moderation

The earth is commonly represented as humanity's bountiful mother, nourishing us with her goodness. In reality, the relationship is very different. Our planet is not a horn of plenty - the resources it offers are limited by its capacity to renew them.

Fresh water, forests and agricultural products are all renewable, provided they are not consumed faster than they can regenerate. Fossil fuels and minerals, by contrast, are finite. Although the effects of overexploitation tend to be felt locally, economic globalisation and international trade in natural resources make this a planetary issue.

Food resources

Food, water and forests are all renewable, but only up to a point. The 'production' of fish, for instance, has grown faster than Europe's population. The global catch has risen from 22 million tons a year in 1950 to 100 million tons now. Average fish consumption in 1950 was 9 kg per person, compared to 19 kg by the beginning of the 1990s. Nevertheless, the fishing industry has fallen into decline as the sea can no longer sustain exploitation at this level.

Cereal production tripled between 1950 and 1990 as agriculture grew steadily more intensive (producing more on less land). Output increased faster than the population, which meant some European agricultural land had to be taken out of cultivation. To say nothing of the ecological implications of these new agricultural practices, which are synonymous with fertilisers, pesticides and soil depletion. Nor do these statistics reflect the immense regional disparities that exist. Many countries have yet to achieve self-sufficiency in food.

The earth : keeping the balance

The earth itself is a fragile inheritance that we must protect from abuse. The pollution generated by agriculture, transport and industry, for instance, affects the balance of the biosphere far beyond the areas in which it is generated. As we approach the year 2000, humanity can no longer

Water and forests

- Europe has 8% of the world's renewable fresh water resources but is responsible for 15% of consumption.
- Although Europe (not including the former USSR) had an extra 1.9 million hectares of forest and woodland in 1990 compared to 1981, atmospheric pollution is a major contributor to loss and damage.

afford to waste resources, whether they be minerals, food, our natural heritage or the space in which we live and work. The globalisation of the economy makes this a planetary issue.

Source : Benelux Press

Europe in action
Objectives and resolutions

The Fifth Environmental Action Programme sets out Europe's strategy for the coming years. It is primarily concerned with our natural resources and their sustainability. The programme focuses on:
- *better management of resources* by industry and more rigorous common standards for manufacturing processes and consumer information;
- tax breaks to promote enhanced energy efficiency and the development of *renewable energy sources*;
- *conservation of natural resources* by the agricultural sector, first and foremost by dealing with the problem of nitrates and pesticides.

Fishing in the North Sea. Source : Frank Spooner Pictures.

A legal framework for renewable resources

Europe's common fishing policy has shown how measures can be taken to protect natural resources. It sets out to achieve the conservation and balanced exploitation of our fish stocks.

Forestry activities have generally been growing over the past twenty years, during which time the area of the planet covered by forest and woodland has decreased by around 6%. Once again, the figures disguise a number of sharp regional disparities. Forestation in the northern temperate zones has increased by 5%, thanks to reforestation and a 10% increase in the forested area of the Europe of the 15.

'Green' label to protect our natural resources

A European eco-label will be awarded to products that do not pollute and which make sparing use of raw materials. Kitchen roll and toilet paper, for instance, will be able to show the eco-label if they:
- use fewer non-renewable resources;
- limit the spread of pollutants in the air and water;
- can be readily recycled.
The eco-label will help consumers to choose everyday products that make more sparing use of our natural resources

Floatings logs. Sources : Stock Imagery.

Tropical rainforests, by contrast, shrank by 50% between 1981 and 1990.

European activities to encourage the rational exploitation of our forests are limited at present to research and the exchange of information. Legislation has, however, been introduced to:
- protect Europe's forests from atmospheric pollution,
- create a European forestry information and communication system.

Although tropical deforestation doesn't have a direct, short-term impact on the European environment, it nevertheless poses a general long-term threat. Europe itself contributes to deforestation through its demand for wood, although imports of the varieties in question have been cut by half over the past 20 years. The Community is currently preparing new rules to meet the objectives set out at Rio.

The Community is also concerned about the impact of agriculture on soil and water reserves. Its main goal in this area is to:
- protect soil whenever sewage sludge is used in agriculture,
- prevent water being polluted by agricultural nitrates.

Nature protection begins with the study and classification of natural habitats and wildlife. There is no shortage of local data, but this is not always comparable at European level because of a lack of compatibility. To deal with this situation, the Community has set up inventory programmes to take stock of our natural heritage based on a common nomenclature of European natural habitats. This is also the first step towards the creation of the Natura 2000 network which will give urgently needed protection to important European natural sites.

Taking responsability

The world

The globalisation of economies and trade has made natural resources an international issue. Food resources are a case in point. Although world food production is growing, there are acute regional differences. The GATT organisation set out to liberalise and harmonise import controls and to give all its member nations the chance to trade fairly. The process was blocked for a considerable time by disagreements on agriculture between the European Community, the United States and a group of countries that supported the total abolition of agricultural subsidies. The conclusion of the Uruguay Round led to GATT's replacement by the new World Trade Organisation.

Source : Benelux Press

Europe and its Member States

The European Community has already made changes to its agricultural policy with less emphasis on subsidising production and more on environmentally friendly farming practices.

Member States are helping to establish the new support system by setting up local programmes that reflect the diversity of Europe's environment, natural conditions and agricultural structures. Farmers are being compensated for lost revenues arising from reduced production and/or increased costs and for their role in improving the environment.

Economic globalisation also has implications for non-renewable raw materials. For the most part, the countries of Europe have long since exhausted their own fuel and mineral reserves and are now dependent on other countries for their supplies (with all the geopolitical and strategic problems that can entail). But reserves throughout the world are finite, too. Exploration for new reserves and the eking out of existing ones by recycling simply delays the inevitable. Europe recognised this fact when it introduced new, more efficient energy management measures after the First Oil Crisis.

More rational town and country planning

Changes in land-use often cause immense ecological upheaval. Human activities affect the environment both directly (mines, dikes, canalisation of rivers) and indirectly (urbanisation, intensive agriculture). They can also transform landscapes by deforestation, desertification and soil erosion. Many European countries have been aware of these issues for many years and have created the tools they need to manage land-use in a rational way.

OPEN HERE

Glossary of terms used

• **TERM**
EXPLANATION

• **acid deposit**
acid atmospheric pollutants which are deposited in dry or wet form

• **acid rain**
rain containing a high acid concentration (sulphurous, sulphuric, nitric) caused by air pollution, which damages historic buildings and poisons plants and animals

• **acidification**
change in an environment's natural chemical balance caused by an increase in the concentration of acidic elements

• **afforestation**
creation of a forest on land that has not previously, at least in recent times, had a significant tree population

• **antimony**
chemical element, brittle, silver coloured, similar to arsenic

• **aquifer**
subterranean body of water filling the spaces in porous and permeable rock and resting on an impermeable layer

• **asbesto**
fibrous natural product used in asbestos cement, brakes and clutches, insulators and fireproof textiles. Asbestos is carcinogenic

• **autochton species**
species originating from the region in which it lives

• **avifauna**
totality of bird-life in a given region

• **benzene**
colourless liquid, insoluble in water and inflammable, which is added to petrol as an antiknock agent.

• **biocenosis**
totality of living organisms, animal and plant, which occupy the same geographical area (biotope)

• **biocide**
chemical product intended for the destruction of living organisms harmful to agriculture

• **biodiversity**
overall diversity of species in the living world, each of which is genetically different and helps ensure the balance of the biosphere

• **biological diversity**
see biodiversity

• **biomass**
total mass of living matter, animal and plant, present at a given place and a given time. Expressed as dry weight

• **biomass fuel**
plant-based fuel

• **biosphere**
the part of the terrestrial sphere made up of living organisms

• **biotechnology**
laboratory technology designed to stimulate and control the transformation of an organic substance using the action of micro-organisms with a view to industrial application

• **biotope**
well-defined geographical area, characterised by specific ecological conditions (soil, climate, etc.), which physically supports the organisms that live there (biocenosis)

• **boreal**
relating to the northern hemisphere, comprising the North Pole and the neighbouring regions - opposite of 'austral'

• **cadmium**
shiny white metal, product of zinc mining, used to make yellow pigments and miniature batteries. Toxic

• **catalytic converter**
vehicle exhaust system which uses catalysis (a process for altering the speed of a chemical reaction) to reduce the emission of pollutants

• **chemical buffer**
solution or substance which maintains a constant rate of acidity

• **chlorofluorocarbon**
gas still used in some aerosols, fridges, air-conditioning units and fire-extinguishers and blamed for depleting the ozone layer

• **composting**
biological process encouraging the fermentation of a variety of organic waste to obtain compost, a mix rich in minerals and organic matter

• **crop rotation**
the sequence of crops to be grown on the same piece of land

• **decibel**
unit of sound measurement

• **defoliation**
natural or disease-related shedding of leaves

• **deforestation**
human destruction of forests

• **degasification**
mechanical or chemical extraction of gases dissolved in water

• **dioxin**
by-product of the manufacture of certain pesticides. Highly toxic and persistent

• **drainage basin**
natural geographical region drained by one or more rivers and their tributaries

• **eco-label**
ecological label awarded to a product that does not harm the environment

• **eco-product**
product designed and manufactured in a way that respects the environment

• **ecosystem**
biological unit formed by the living environment and the animal and plant organisms that live in it

• **effluent**
in ecological terms, any liquid produced by an industrial process

• **endemic**
description of a living species confined to a particular region

• **environmental impact assessment**
study which systematically describes and evaluates the environmental consequences of a development project (road, factory, etc.)

• **environmental label**
see eco-label

• **eutrophication**
accumulation of organic matter in water, resulting in deoxygenation (reduction in the water's oxygen content)

- **fallow**
the status of a piece of arable land taken temporarily out of cultivation

- **fauna**
totality of animal species present within a specific biotope

- **fermentation**
breakdown of organic matter by the action of enzymes secreted by microscopic organisms

- **fertilisation**
operation designed to maintain or improve the fertility of a soil by the addition of fertiliser

- **flora**
totality of plant species present in a region or biotope

- **food chain**
succession of living organisms, each of which feeds on others according to a fixed order

- **fossil energy**
see fossil fuel

- **fossil fuel**
natural carbon substance produced by the breakdown of organic matter buried in layers deep in the earth's crust. Forms include gaseous fuels (natural gas), liquids (oil, asphalt) and solids (coal)

- **gene**
segment of the deoxyribonucleic acid (DNA) molecule located at a specific point of a chromosome, responsible for determining an inherited characteristic

- **genetic**
scientific study of the laws of heredity

- **genetic engineering**
totality of techniques for modifying the genetic programme of certain living cells (bacteria) to enable them to manufacture useful substances, the manufacture of which would be difficult or impossible

- **geological layer**
homogeneous sedimentary deposit

- **greenhouse gas**
gas (carbon dioxide, nitrogen dioxide, methane, water vapour, etc.) which contributes to the greenhouse effect, i.e. the heating up of the lower atmosphere by trapping solar rays

- **ground cover**
totality of small herbaceous and woody plants which cover an area of soil, protecting it from temperature variations and erosion

- **groundwater**
layer of subterranean water, generally close to the surface, which supplies wells and springs

- **habitat**
ecological setting in which an organism, species, population or group of species lives

- **half-life**
period in which a physical or biological quantity reaches half of its initial value

- **heavy metal**
metal which becomes toxic in high concentrations. Heavy metals can accumulate within the food chain (lead, cadmium, mercury, etc.)

- **humus**
organic matter formed from plant and animal debris or other organic substances that collect on or in the soil

- **hydro-electricity**
electricity generated by harnessing the hydraulic energy of rivers and waterfalls

- **hydrocarbon**
organic compound made up of carbon and hydrogen. Oil and natural gas are basically hydrocarbon compounds

- **industrial wastewaters**
water carrying wastes and effluents produced by industrial plants

- **input**
element used to produce a good

- **insularisation**
geographical isolation

- **land use planning**
organisation of space in such a way as to improve living conditions, encourage economic development and make optimum use of natural resources without disrupting natural ecosystems

- **leached**
description of soil into which water has carried soluble or colloidal substances

- **lead-poisoning**
toxic effects of lead or lead salts

- **lifecycle**
the total life of a product, from manufacture to final disposal

- **liquid manure**
natural fertiliser based on animal dung and containing a large amount of water

- **methane**
colourless gas given off by rotting materials. The main constituent of natural gas

- **microclimate**
climate peculiar to a small area, dependent on local vegetation, microrelief, etc.

- **monoculture**
cultivation of a single plant variety

- **mutagenic**
description of a chemical or physical agent capable of causing mutations within a species

- **mutation**
sudden and permanent change in the structure of a gene or chromosome. May occur spontaneously or may be caused by the action of one or more mutagens

- **nitrate**
the main source of nitrogen for plants

- **nitrogenous fertiliser**
fertiliser containing nitrogen in the form of nitrates or ammonia

- **non-waste technology**
technology causing little pollution

- **nutrient**
element that can be assimilated by an organism without being transformed by the digestive system. A distinction is made between macronutrients like calcium, nitrogen and phosphorous and micronutrients like copper, zinc and manganese

- **ocean floor**
solid layer located at the bottom of oceans and seas. Comprises the oceanic crust covered with a thick layer of sediment

- **offshore exploitation**
operation of an oil-well located off the coast

- **overgrazing**
excessive grazing which prevents the regeneration of undergrowth, reduces the productive potential of plant species and sometimes encou-

rages soil degradation through erosion

- **ozone**
simple gaseous compound which forms a protective layer in the upper atmosphere shielding the earth from certain forms of solar radiation. In the lower atmosphere, by contrast, ozone is a pollutant

- **pathogenic**
description of an agent that induces illness

- **peat bog**
acidic peat environment typical of wetlands. Peat bogs are colonised by characteristic low vegetation including moss, rushes and heather

- **percolation**
flow of rain or irrigation water (percolate) through cracks in the soil under the influence of gravity

- **pesticide**
chemical compound designed to destroy animal or plant pests. May be an insecticide, herbicide or fungicide. Pesticides accumulate in the food chain, contaminating food supplies and groundwater

- **phosphorus**
mineral vital to the growth of living organisms

- **phytoplankton**
totality of single or multi-celled plant organisms which live suspended in sea and freshwater

- **piscicultural**
concerned with fish-farming

- **precautionary principle**
the principe according to which the necessary measures should be taken once a sufficient level of probability is reached, even in the absence of scientific certainty

- **purification**
operation to remove impurities from wastewater

- **radioactive cloud**
cloud of solid particles formed in the wake of a nuclear detonation or the emission of radioactive substances into the atmosphere following an explosion at a nuclear power plant

- **radioactivity**
spontaneous emission of radiation, normally alpha or beta par-

ticles often accompanied by gamma rays, from the nucleus of an (unstable) isotope. As a result of this emission the radioactive isotope is transformed into the isotope of another element which can also be radioactive (it decays). Ultimately, as the result of one more phases of radioactivity decay, a stable (non-radioactive) end products is formed.

- **reforestation**
the reconstitution of a forest

- **renewable energy**
energy, the consumption of which does not reduce natural resources because it is based on elements that replenish themselves naturally (biomass, solar, wind, geothermal and hydro power)

- **river contract**
agreement between all relevant public and private bodies concerning the natural functions of waterways, their maintenance and use (sanitary, cultural, economic and recreational)

- **salmonellosis**
infection caused by bacteria (salmonellae) including typhoid and paratyphoid fevers and gastro-enteritis

- **sediment**
granular deposit left by water, wind and other agents of erosion

- **seismicity**
number and intensity of earth tremors in a given region and period of time

- **silty**
describes a high content of silt. Silt is a form of earth with the consistency of flour - light but sticky, somewhere between sand and clay

- **silvicultural**
concerning forestry

- **silviculture**
totality of rules and techniques allowing the cultivation, maintenance and exploitation of a forest

- **smog**
type of fog caused by the atmospheric emission of gaseous or vehicular pollutants

- **soil amendment**
operation designed to improve the physical properties of a soil - substance added to soil for this purpose

- **solvent**
liquid used to dissolve an active substance

- **spawning ground**
place where fish come together to reproduce

- **species**
totality of like individuals which transmit their likeness from one generation to another

- **spraying**
the regular spraying of a substance or product on the surface of the soil (fertiliser, wastewater) or on a crop or tree population (pesticides)

- **stratosphere**
part of the earthís atmosphere located at an altitude between 12 and 50 km. The temperature of the stratosphere rises with altitude

- **suspended solids**
microscopic particles of matter in water. Can be removed by settlement or filtration

- **thermal barrier**
barrier of a thermal character. for example, a thermal barrier limits the geographical expansion of a species

- **to clear, to grub**
to clear a piece of land by removing all the undergrowth, either by uprooting or burning

- **wastewater treatment plant**
totality of installations and devices used to purify wastewaters and industrial effluents to allow them to be reused or released into the environment

- **wastewaters**
generic term covering household effluent, residues and drainwater

- **weathering**
totality of phenomena affecting the earth's relief (ice, wind, rain)

GLOSSARY

- **ACRONYMS AND ABBREVIATIONS** : *EXPLANATION*

- **ACP :** African, Caribbean and Pacific (countries)

- **AMAP :** Arctic Monitoring and Assessment Programme

- **ANC :** Acid Neutralising Capacity

- **AQG :** Air Quality Guidelines (of WHO)

- **BaP** : Benzo(a)pyrene

- **BOD** : Biochemical Oxygen Demand

- **CAP** : Common Agricultural Policy (EU)

- **CFC** : Chlorofluorocarbon

- **CFP** : Common Fisheries Policy (EU)

- **CH$_4$** : Methane

- **CLP** : Chlorine Loading Potential

- **CO$_2$** : Carbon Dioxide

- **COD** : Chemical Oxygen Demand

- **CORINE** : CO-oRdination of INformation on the Environment (CEC)

- **CSD** : Commission on Sustainable Development (UN)

- **DDT** : Dichloryldiphenyltrichorethane

- **DG** : Directorate General of European Commission

- **DMS** : Dimethylsulphide

- **DNA** : Desoxyribonucleic acid

- **EASOE** : European Arctic Stratospheric Ozone Experiment

- **EBCC** : European Bird Census Council

- **EBRD** : European Bank for Reconstruction and Development

- **EC** : European Community

- **ECCC** : European Coastal Conservation Conference

- **ECE** : Economic Commission for Europe (UN)

- **ECEH** : European Centre for Environmental Health (WHO)

- **EEA(-TF)** : European Environment Agency (Task Force, CEC DG XI)

- **EFTA :** European Free Trade Association

- **EIA** : Environmental Impact Assessment

- **EINECS** : European Inventory of Existing Chemical Substances (CEC)

- **EOAC** : European Ornithological Atlas Committee

- **ESA** : Environmentally Sensitive Area

- **EU** : European Union

- **FAO** : Food and Agriculture Organization (UN)

- **FCCC :** Framework Convention on Climate Change (UN)

- **FGD** : Flue-Gas Desulphurisation

- **FOREGS** : Forum of European Geological Surveys

- **gamma-HCH** : Lindane (organochlorine pesticide) (= gamma hexachlorohexane)

- **GATT** : General Agreement on Tariffs and Trade

- **GDP** : Gross Domestic Product

- **GEF** : Global Environmental Facility

- **GESAMP** : Group of Experts on the Scientific Aspects of Marine Pollution

- **GFCM** : General Fisheries Council for the Mediterranean

- **GMO :** Genetically Modified Organism

- **GMP** : Gross Material Product

- **GNP** : Gross National Product

- **GWP** : Global Warming Potential

- **H$_2$O$_2$** : Hydrogen peroxide

- **HCFC** : Hydrochlorofluorocarbon

- **HGWP** : Halocarbon Global Warming Potential

- **IAEA** : International Atomic Energy Agency (UN)

- **ICBP** : International Council for Bird Preservation (now BirdLife International)

- **ICES** : International Council for the Exploration of the Sea

- **IEA** : International Energy Agency (UN)

- **IPCS** : International Programme on Chemical Safety (WHO, UNEP, ILO)

- **MAP** : Mediterranean Action Plan

- **MPC** : Maximum permissible concentration

- **MSY** : Maximum sustainable yield

- **NGO** : Non-Governmental Organisation

- **NMVOC** : Non-Methane Volatile Organic Compound

- **N$_2$O** : Dinitrogen oxide (traditionally called nitrous oxide)

- **NO** : Nitrogen oxide (traditionally called nitric oxide)

- **NO$_2$** : Nitrogen dioxide

- **NO$_x$** : Nitrogen oxides (non-specific, including NO and NO2)

- **OECD** : Organization for Economic Cooperation and Development

- **OH** : Hydroxyl

- **ODP** : Ozone Depletion Potential

- **PAH** : Polycyclic (or polynuclear) Aromatic Hydrocarbon

- **PAN** : Peroxyacetylnitrate

- **PCB** : Polychlorinated biphenyl

- **PCDD** : Polychlorinated dibenzodioxin

- **PCDF** : Polychlorinated dibenzofuran

- **POCP** : Photochemical Ozone Creation Potential

- **POP** : Persistent Organic Pollutants

- **SO$_2$** : Sulphur dioxide

- **TOE** : Tonnes of Oil Equivalent

- **UNCED** : United Nations Conference on Environment and Development (Rio de Janeiro, June 1992, 'the Earth summit')

- **UNESCO** : United Nations Educational Scientific and Cultural Organization

- **USSR** : Union of Soviet Socialist Republics

- **VOC** : Volatile Organic Compound

- **WHO** : World Health Organization (UN)

- **5th Environmental Action Programme**
  CE. Bruxelles, 1993
  Official Journal of the European Communities
  C138 p1-98

- **Towards sustainability**
  The European Commission's progress report and action plan on the fifth programme of policy and action in relation to the environment and sustainable development.
  European Communities, Luxembourg, 1997.

- **Environment in the European Union - 1995 Report for the review of the Fifth Environmental Action Programme**
  EEA, Copenhagen, 1995,
  151p

- **Europe's Environment - The Dobris Assessment**
  EEA, Copenhagen, 1995 dl,
  676p.

- **Europe's Environment - Statistical Compendium for the Dobris Assessment**
  Eurostat, Luxembourg, 1995.

- **Europe's Environment - The Dobris Assessment - An overview**
  EEA, Copenhagen, 1994 dl.,
  22p.

- **Europeans and the Environment in 1995 (Eurobarometer 43.1 bis)**
  DGXI, Brussels, 1995,
  84p

- **Environmental Policy of the European Communities, 2nd ed.**
  Kluwer Law, The Hague, 1995

- **Europe in Figures**
  Eurostat, Luxembourg, 4th ed., 1995,
  425p.

- **Environment and Health in Europe**
  EEA/WHO, 1996

- **Sources**
  The texts of the various EC Directives and regulations are published in the Official Journal of the European Communities. They are also available on the CELEX database.

- For further details contact your local office of the European Commission or one of the sales offices mentioned at the back of the book.

European Communities -
Commission

CARING FOR OUR FUTURE
ACTION FOR EUROPE'S ENVIRONMENT

Luxembourg :
Office for Official Publications
of the European Communities
1998

140 pp.
21.0 x 29.7 cm

ISBN 92-828-2889-1

Price (excluding VAT)
in Luxembourg :
ECU 20